SCHOOL HOUSE BOOKS
Practical Guide
to the
Advanced Placement

English Literature and Composition
Examination

by
Duane Earnest
English Instructor
Detroit Lakes Community
Senior High School

SECOND EDITION

SCHOOL HOUSE BOOKS
921 Pembina Trail
Detroit Lakes, Minnesota 56501

Acknowledgments

This book is dedicated to my wife, Julia Lucca Earnest, for her support and encouragement, and to my three daughters: Crystal Earnest, who is soon to be an English teacher herself, Bridgette Earnest, who is a senior in college majoring in elementary education, and Erin Earnest, who will graduate from high school this year. They have all inspired me to be a better teacher.

I would also like to thank Lowell Niklaus, Mary Regelstad, and Rod Thompson, for their continued administrative support, as well as my fellow English teachers: Jack Archer, Sandy Burd, Jennifer Burnside, Sylvia Fleming, Mark Hassenstab, Dennis Kral, Elaine Meyer, Barb Oistad, and Rebecca Weets. They have all had a tremendous influence on my professional life.

Author: Duane Earnest

Publisher: SCHOOL HOUSE BOOKS

Text Cover: Nicholas and Crystal Bieter
St. Paul, MN

Editor: Joseph Legeuri
Mesabi East High School
Aurora, Minnesota

ISBN 1 - 928741 - 01 - 0

SECOND EDITION

For information write: SCHOOL HOUSE BOOKS
921 Pembina Trail
Detroit Lakes, MN 56501

Publications from the AP College Board have been the major source of reference for writing this book. Authors from the AP Suggested Reading List have been categorized by time period. Checklists for grading essays have been compiled by examining the rubrics used to grade previous essays. Inferences have been made about the types of essay and multiple-choice questions by examining the previous tests given. Practice tests have been compiled using previous AP tests as models. All these AP publications can be obtained by writing to The Advanced Placement Program, P.O. Box 6670, Princeton, New Jersey 08541-6670.

Student Acknowledgments

Thanks to the following students for their invaluable help in finding passages, writing questions, grading papers, and field-testing all exams:

Jessica Abrahams, Karla Ash, Sarah Augustin, Sarah Baker, Mikk Bakker, Heidi Bauer, Krista Benson, Jennifer Birzneiks, Kara Birznieks, Erin Block, Nick Bowers, Jaime Bruflodt, Devon Brenk, Jade Buermann, Dave Burlingame, Luke Burroughs, Casey Cannon, Amy Cornelius, Lori Dahring, Erin Earnest, Lisa Eidenschink, Randy Fairbanks, Jenny Flottemesch, Emily Fishback, Amy Friendshuh, Andrea Grabow, Jolynn Garnes, Lindsey Gunderson, Charlie Haggart, Katie Hagle, Nerissa Haisley, Magan Hanlon, Alyssa Haspel, Reid Heckman, Kent Heimark, Micah Heisler, Nick Heisserer, Eric Heyer, Shanda Hochstetler, Kent Hoeglund, Nels Hoplin, Derek Hopper, Kristen Husby, Jenny Hutchinson, Phillip Imholte, Nathan Ittner, Jenni Jacobs, Shane Jahnke, Sarah Jensen, Erica Johnson, Kristina Johnson, Lindsey Johnson, Joni Johnston, Erin Jorgenson, Tony King, Kadie Kippen, Amanda Kittleson, Becky Koshnik, Ryan Kotta, Abby Kovala, Alissa Kovala, Jake Laabs, Dan Lee, Chris Lahren, Birk Larsen, Amy Lehrke, Liz Linquist, Greg Luhman, Jena Lund, Jill Mack, Jodi Mallow, Ben Matter, Jay Matter, Angie McKenzie, Cassie Meyer, Mike Miller, Josie Musquiz, Kara Nelson, Becky Newton, Renae Niklaus, Matt Nustad, Angie Nyland, Amy Olson, Billi Jo Olson, Lisa Olson, Britton O'Neill, Sarah Orvik, Leslie Parker, Stacey Pavelko, Erin Pentinnen, Chris Perry, Anna Potvin, Steph Rasmussen, Tim Refsland, Ruth Rhoades, Erin Rogers, Jessica Rogers, Karly Russness, Anita Salmela, Naomi Salmela, Erik Scharrer, Kelly Schlauderaff, Kelly Scmit, Steph Schmitz, Adam Schneider, Kris Seabloom, Erin Seaworth, Stephanie Shoemaker, Katy Skogmo, Becky Sletto, Mary Solie, Tina Sonnenberg, Joe Starkey, Adam Steffl, Kelli Steffl, Jill Steinmetz, Tracy Stoltenburg, Anne Stowman, Annie Swanberg, Nate Swanberg, Terri Sundbom, Gabe Sunram, Rick Swensen, Tina Taves, Matt Taylor, Marit Thorsgard, Sally Tovson, Michelle Tucker, Tiffany Turnwall, Robert Wagner, Luke Weekley, Jill White, Wade Whitworth, Lisa Windloss, Laurie Wolfe, Jill Wothe, Betsy Zeman, and Renee Zeeman.

Table of Contents

Preface

The following *Practical Guide to the Advanced Placement English Literature and Composition Examination* is designed to be used as a complement to the already existing excellent literature classes throughout the United States. It is designed to be used in the hands of the students as a resource, as a guide to enrich existing curriculum, making it more AP specific. Using this text in this way, the student will learn to read more perceptively and write more maturely — an honorable goal for any English instruction.

I wrote this book in conjunction with the writing of *A Practical Guide to the Advanced Placement English Language and Composition Examination*. Works read in Language and Composition are studied in terms mainly of their rhetorical merit — how the authors manipulate the language to convey their attitude or purpose, or to create an effect. Works read in Literature and Composition are studied in terms mainly of their literary merit — how the authors manipulate the plot, conflict, setting, and characterization to create theme. Because of this difference, the Language Revision chapter in the AP Language Guide has been replaced by separate chapters here in Poetry, Prose, and Drama. Other differences between the two examinations are specifically addressed in each of the appropriate chapters.

All inferences made are based on my examinations of various AP Literature publications and tests given from 1970 to 1999. I designed AP essay questions on materials I was teaching, developed checklists for grading essays by examining rubrics used to grade previous essays, and wrote full-length multiple-choice tests using previously published AP Literature tests as models. With each task, I was able to make predictions about AP Literature expectations. This book is a result of those studies.

Chapter One: Suggested Reading

New to this edition, this chapter has arranged some of the most highly recommended writers by author's name, title, and time period. These works have appeared on various lists and tests created by the AP program and most have won various book awards. Whenever possible, read authors from each of the time periods; read a good selection of female and multi-cultural writers; read a good variety of genres, etc. Reading a wide variety of works literary merit, like those on this list, is the best way to ensure success on either of the English tests.

Chapter Two: The Essay

The Essay section offers a detailed analysis of the types of questions asked since 1970, strategy suggestions for writing various types of style analyses and open essays, and checklists and rubrics for each type of question asked.

Students Grading Students

Seven years ago I decided that I would have my students grade each others' papers in a reader's response fashion. I spent much time in the beginning teaching them to be positive in their remarks. Once this message was understood, the students had difficulty being critical enough. Without objective direction, I began to realize my experiment with student grading was failing. My students were feeling great about themselves, but their writing was getting worse!

Turning to the rubrics created by the College Board to grade previous AP essays, I discovered that each set of descriptions had nine distinct elements. By putting these in the form of checklists, I now had a vehicle for my students to use in effectively grading other papers on the nine point scale used by AP. Each essay written is now graded by three people — two students and me. I grade them holistically, putting a mark of 1 - 9 in my grade book. Once they receive a paper to grade, students refer to the checklists on pp. 38-51. Using these as a guide, they fill out a generic cover sheet (see pp. 38-39 in Chapter Two or see the separate Teacher's Guide Addendum) naming the type of essay, checking appropriate items and making reader's responses, ultimately arriving at a mark of 1 - 9. Using the checklists has been the key to effective student grading. Using the checklists as a guide, the reader responses are still friendly, but they are now also more critically appropriate than the "Nice job, Joe!" responses I was getting earlier.

This system of checklists also encourages much beneficial dialogue. If the graders' marks vary more than two points from mine, I check with the graders. Once the students get their own papers back, they are allowed to negotiate the score with me whenever they can defend parts of their paper that deserve a better grade. I now spend less time reading papers and more time talking about papers. My students now benefit with improved writing skills.

Chapter Three: Multiple Choice

The Multiple Choice section offers strategy suggestions for taking tests, and a detailed analysis of the types of questions AP asks. The information in this chapter allows students and teachers to collaboratively write multiple choice questions for any materials taught.

Chapter Four - Poetry
Chapter Five - Prose
Chapter Six - Drama

These chapters are devoted to helping students become better readers by providing them with the right types of questions to ask. These types of questions appear in many textbooks. The questions in these chapters, however, are arranged in a three-step close reading approach to aid the student in brainstorming and eventually writing the type of essays required by the Advanced Placement Literature examination. This three step approach is as follows:

1. What is the meaning?
2. How do the language devices create meaning?
3. So what?

Chapter Seven: Creative Suggestions

Contests, games, and other creations !

Chapter Eight: Writing Prompts

Various types of formal, informal, long term, and impromptu writing .

Chapter Nine: Glossary

Advanced Placement terms defined.

Chapter Ten: Three NEW Full-Length Practice Tests

Sample essays, rubrics, and multiple-choice tests that are included have been compiled by my students through my guidance. These tests were field tested by my students. After taking the tests, we changed the wording of those questions which most people got wrong. The multiple-choice section tests vocabulary, point of view, pronoun reference, meaning, rhetoric, diction, sentence structure, effect, tone, and organization. I use these tests at various times throughout the year to measure my students' learning. They can either be given in one three-hour sitting, or separately within the t of the regular classroom.

Test Results

Each sample test ends with the checklists, rubrics, and results of essay writing. I chose to exclude answers and explanations for the three full multiple-choice tests because I wanted these to be used as graded tests in my classroom. These answers and explanations are available in a separate teacher's key.

This book is designed to be a companion textbook to the excellent curriculums already taught in AP classrooms around the country. In the hands of each student, this book can ensure more success in the AP classroom, giving students the potential to succeed on the eventual AP English Literature and Composition exam, and ultimately, helping students to become better prepared for college courses.

Chapter One: Suggested Reading- Literature and Composition AP

Plays of Literary Merit
Written Before 1900

Aeschylus, *Oresteia. Agamemmon. The Libation Bearers.*
      The Eumenides.
Oliver Goldsmith, *The Vicar of Wakefield. She Stoops to Conquer.*
Victor Hugo, *Les Miserables.*
Ben Johnson, *Works* (A Collection of Plays and Poems)
Euripides, *Medea.*
Christopher Marlowe, *Dr. Faustus.*
Moliere, *Tartuffe. The Misanthrope.*
William Shakespeare, *As You Like It. Hamlet. Romeo and*
      Juliet. The Turn of the Screw. Twelfth Night. Othello.
      King Lear. A Midsummer Night's Dream.
      Anthony and Cleopatra. The Merchant of Venice.
      Henry IV.
Sophocles, *Oedipus the King. Oedipus Rex. Antigone.*

Plays of Literary Merit
Written in the Twentieth Century

Edward Albee, *Who's Afraid of Virginia Woolf?*
Samuel Beckett, *Waiting for Godot. Krapp's Last Tape.*
Anton Chekov, *The Sea Gull. Uncle Vanga. The Three Sisters.*
      The Cherry Orchard.
Rita Dove, *The Darker Face of the Earth.*
Lorraine Hainsberry, *A Raisin in the Sun.*
Lillian Hellman, *The Children's Hour. The Little Foxes.*
      The Autumn Garden. Watch on the Rhine.
      Toys in the Attic.
Davis Henry Hwang, *M. Butterfly.*
Henrik Ibsen, *A Doll House.*
W. Inge, *Come Back, Little Sheba.*
Eugene Ionesco, *The Bald Soprano.*
Arthur Miller, *The Crucible. Death of a Salesman.*
      All My Sons.
Sean O'Casey, *Juno and the Paycock. The Shadow of a Gunman.*
      The Plough and the Stars.
Eugene O'Neill, *Beyond the Horizon.*
      Long Day's Journey Into Night. Iceman Cometh.

Harold Pinter, *The Caretaker. The Homecoming. Betrayal.*
     Old Times. The Birthday Party. Landscape.
     The Dumb Waiter.
Luigi Pirandello, *Naked Masks (Five Plays).*
George Bernard Shaw, *Pygmalion. Mrs. Warren's Profession.*
     Saint Joan.
Sam Shepard, *Buried Child.*
Richard Brinsley Sheridan, *The Rivals. The Scvhool for Scandal.*
Tom Stoppard, *Rosencrantz and Guildenstern Are Dead.*
Oscar Wilde, *The Importance of Being Earnest.*
Thornton Wilder, *Our Town.*
Tennesee Williams, *A Street Car Named Desire.*
     The Glass Menagerie, Summer and Smoke.
     Cat on a Hot Tin Roof. A Lovely Sunday for Creve Coeur.
August Wilson, *Fences. The Piano Lesson.*

Poetry Collections
or "Titles of Longer Poems"
of Literary Merit
Written Before 1900

William Blake, *The Complete Poetry and Prose of William Blake.*
Anne Bradstreet, Various Anthologies.
Robert Browning, *The Poetical Works of Robert Browning.*
     Complete from 1833 to 1868.
Lord Byron, *The Poetical Works of Byron.*
Geoffrey Chaucer, "Canterbury Tales."
Samuel Taylor Coleridge, "The Rime of the Ancient Mariner."
     "Cristabel." and "Kubla Khan."
     Poems of Samuel Taylor Coleridge.
Emily Dickinson, *Poems and Letters of Emily Dickinson.*
John Donne, *The Poetry of Johh Donne.*
Homer, *The Odyssey.*
Gerald Manley Hopkins, *A Hopkins Reader.*
John Keats, *Selected Poems.*
Robert Lowell, *Prometheus Bound.*
John Milton, *The Complete English Poietry Of John Milton.*
     L'allegro.
Edgar Allan Poe, *An Edgar Allan Poe Reader: Poems and Short*
     Stories. Essay and Reviews: Theory of Poetry.

Alexander Pope, "Rape of the Lock."
> *The Complete Poeticxal Works of Alexander Pope.*

William Shakespeare, *The Complete Works of William Shakespeare.*

Alfred Lord Tennyson, *Selections from Tennyson and Browning.*
> "The Charge of the Light Brigade."

Virgil, *The Aeneid.*

Walt Whitman, *Leaves of Grass.*

William Wordsworth, *The Complete Poetical Works*
> *of William Wordsworth.*

William Butler Yeats, *Collected Poems.*

Poetry Collections
or "Titles of Longer Poems"
of Literary Merit
Written in the Twentieth Century

African American Voices (A collection of writings by such
> authors as W. E. B. Dubois, Toni Morrison,
> Rita Dove, Richard Wright, and Ralph Ellison
> exploring the connections of circle, veil, water,
> and song that link past and present African
> American cultures)

W. H. Auden, *Reading from his Works (record).*
> *Collected Shorter Poems, Selected Poems.*
> *The Dog Beneath the Skin. About the House.*

Mayou Angelou, *Just Give Me a Cool Drink of Water 'fore I Diiie.*
> *Oh Pray My Wings Are Going To Fit Me Well.*
> *And Still I Rise. Shaker Why Don't You Sing.*

The Best American Poetry, Edited by Adrienne Rich

Elizabeth Bishop, *The Complete Poems. Geography III.*
> *Questions of Travel.*

Gwendolyn Brooks, *Beckonings. Bronzeville Boys and Girls.*
> *Gwendolyn Brooks Reading Her Poetry (Record).*

H. D. (Hilda Doolittle), *Collected Poems.*

Rita Dove, Poetry Collections: Pulitzer prize-winning
> "Thomas and Beulah" as well as "Museum" and
> "The Yellow House on the Corner"

T. S. Eliot, *The Complete Poems and Plays of T. S. Eliot.*
> *Old Possum's Book of Practical Cats.*

Collected Poems 1909 - 1962.
Murder in the Cathedral.
"The Love Song of J. Alfred Prufrock,"
"The Waste Land," *On Poetry and Poets* (Essays by
T. S. Eliot).
Robert Frost, *Complete Poems.*
Joy Harjo, *In Mad Love and War.*
Seamus Heaney, *Selected Poems from 1966 to 1987.*
Garrett Hongo, *The Open Boat: Poems from Asian America
with and Introduction from Garrett Hongo.*
A. E. Houseman, *The Collected Poems of A. E. Houseman.*
Langston Hughes, *The Block: Poems. Selected Poems.
The Dream Keeper and Other Poems.*
Phillip Larkin, *The Whitsun Weddings. The Less Deceived.*
D. H. Lawrence, *The Complete Poems of D. H. Lawrence.*
Lean Out the Window (Poetry Selections from Gwendolyn
Brooks, James Joyce, Stephen Vincent Benet, Robert
Frost, Elinor Wylie, Conrad Aitken, etc.)
Marianne Moore, *The Complete Poems of Marianne Moore.
Tell Me, Tell Me; Granite , Steel, and Other Topics.
O To Be A Dragon.*
Gloria Naylor, *Linden Hills.*
Wilfred Owen, *Collected Poems.*
Slyvia Plath, *Crossing the Water - Transitional Poems.
Ariel. The Colossus and Other Poems.*
Adrienne Rich, Collection of Poems: *The Will to Change.
Diving Into the Wreck.
A Wild Patience Has Taken Me This Far.*
Leslie Marmon Silko, *Ceremony.*
Cathy Song, *Picture Bride.*
Six American Poets (Walt Whitman, Emily Dickinson,
Wallace Stevens, William Carlos Williams,
Robert Frost, and Langston Hughes).
Stopping for Death (A collection of poems about death, loss,
and mourning, written by poets from all over the world
including Alice Walker, Janet Frome, and
Seamus Heaney).
Dylan Thomas, *Selections from the Writings of Dylan Thomas.
The Collected Poems.*
Derek Walcott, *Collected Poems. Midsummer.
The Arkansas Testament.*
Walt Whitman, *Leaves of Grass.*
Richard Wilbur, *A Game of Catch. Collected Poems.*
William Carlos Williams, *Selected Poems.*

Works of Literary Merit
Written Before 1900

Louisa May Alcott, *Little Women.*
Jane Austen, *Pride and Predjudice. Sense and Sensibility.*
      Mansfield Park, Emma.
Ambrose Bierce, *The Devil's Dictionary.*
Charlotte Bronte, *Jane Eyre.*
Emily Bronte, *Wuthering Heights.*
Cervantes, *Don Quixote.*
Kate Chopin, *The Awakening,* Two volumes of Short Stories:
      Bayou Folk and *A Night in Arcadie*
Stephen Crane, *The Red Badge of Courage.*
      Maggie: A Girl of the Streets.
Charles Dickens, *A Tale of Two Cities. Great Expectations.*
      Bleak House. Hard Times. Our Mutual Friend.
Fyodor Dostoevski, *Crime and Punishment.*
      The Brothers Karamazov.
George Eliot, *Adam Bede. Silas Marner. The Mill on the Floss.*
      Middlemarch.
Henry Fielding, *Tom Jones.*
Thomas Hardy, *The Return of the Native. Far from the*
      Maddening Crowd. The Mayor of Casterbridge.
      Tess of the T'Urbevilles.
Nathaniel Hawthorne, *The Scarlet Letter. The Custom House.*
      The House of Seven Gables. The Blithedale Romance.
      Marble Faun, Twice-Told Tales.
William Howells, *The Rise of Silas Lapham.*
Herman Melville, *Moby-Dick.*
Edgar Allan Poe, *The Fall of the House of Usher.*
      The Pit and the Pendulum. The Purloined Letter.
      Murders in the Rue Morgue. The Complete Tales
      and Poems of Edgar Allan Poe.
      Selected Prose and Poetry.
Robert Louis Stevenson, *Black Arrow. Dr. Jeckyll and Mr. Hyde.*
Harriet Beecher Stowe, *Uncle Tom's Cabin.*
Jonathan Swift, *Gulliver's Travels.*
Leo Tolstoy, *War and Peace. Anna Karenina.*
Mark Twain, *The Adventures of Huckleberry Finn.*
      Life on the Mississippi. A Connecticut Yankee
      in King Arthur's Court.

Works of Literary Merit
Written in the Twentieth Century

Edward Abby , *Cactus Country.*
Chinua Achebe, *Things Fall Apart.*
James Agee, *A Death in the Family.*
Rudolfo Anaya, *Bless Me, Ultima.*
Gloria Anzaldua, *Borderlands - La Frontera (Prose and Poetry)*
Sherwood Anderson, *Winesburg, Ohio..*
Isaac Asimov, *More Tales of the Black Widowers.*
       The Best of Isaac Asimov.
James Baldwin, *Go Tell It on The Mountain.*
       Notes of a Native Son. Nobody Knows My Name.
       The Fire Next Time. The Price of a Ticket.
       Another Country.
Saul Bellow, *Henderson is the Rain King.*
       The Adventures of Augie March.
Anthony Burgess, *A Clockwork Orange.*
Raymond Carver, Collections of short stories such as:
       Will You Please Be Quiet, Please?
       What We Talk About When We Talk About Love.
       Where I'm Calling From: New And Selected Stories.
Erskine Caldwell, *Tobacco Road.*
James M. Cain, *The Postman Always Rings Twice.*
Wila Cather, *Death Comes for the Archbishop .*
John Cheever, *The Wapshot Chronicles.*
Joseph Conrad, *The Secret Agent. Nostromo. Heart of Darkness.*
       Lord Jim . The Mirror of the Sea (Essays about ships
       and sailors)
Anita Desai, *Fire on the Mountain. Clear Light of Day.*
E. L. Doctorow, *Ragtime.*
J. P. Donnleavy, *The Ginger Man.*
Theodore Drieser, *An American Tragedy. Sister Carrie.*
Lawrence Durell, *The Alexandria Quartet.*
Ralph Ellison, *Invisible Man.*
Louise Erdich, *Love Medicine. The Beet Queen. Tracks.*
       The Crown of Columbus.
William Faulkner, *The Sound and the Fury. As I Lay Dying.*
       Light in August.
James T. Farrell, *The Studs Lonigan Trilogy.*
F. Scott Fitzgerald, *The Great Gatsby. Tender is the Night.*

E. M. Forster, *A Passage to India. Howard's End.*
     A Room With a View. Aspects of the Novel.
John Fowles, *The Magus.*
Robert Graves, *I, Claudius.*
Jack Green, *Loving.*
Graham Grene, *The Power and the Glory.*
Dashiell Hammett, *The Maltese Falcon.*
Joseph Heller, *Catch-22.*
Lillian Hellman, *Pentimento. Scoundrel Time.*
     An Unfinished Woman.
Ernest Hemingway, *The Sun Also Rises. A Farewell to Arms.*
Richard Hughes, *A High Wind in Jamaica.*
Henry James, *Washington Square. The Wings of the Dove.*
     The Ambassadors. The Golden Bowl . Tropic of Cancer.
     Partial Portraits. Daisy Miller.
James Joyce, *Ullysses, A Portrait of the Artist as a Young Man.*
     From Here to Eternity. Finnegan's Wake.
William Kennedy, *Ironweed.*
Joy Kogawa, *Obasan.*
Arthur Koestler, *Darkness at Noon.*
Rudyard Kipling, *Kim.*
D. H. Lawrence, *Sons and Lovers. The Rainbow. Women in Love.*
     Aaron's Rod.
Harper Lee, *To Kill a Mockingbird.*
Sinclair Lewis, *Main Street .*
Jack London, *The Call of the Wild.*
Norman Mailer, The *Naked and the Dead.*
Bernard Malamud, *The Natural. The Assistant. The Fixer.*
     The Tenants.
Katherine Mansfield, *The Short Stories of Kathryn Mansfield.*
Bobbie Ann Mason, *The Rookers.*
W. Somerset Maugham, *Of Human Bondage .*
Cormac McCarthy, *All the Pretty Horses.*
Carson McCullers, *The Heart is a Lonely Hunter.*
N. Scott Momanday, *House Made of Dawn.*
Toni Morrison, *The Bluest Eye. Beloved. Sula.*
Bharati Mukherjee, *Jasmine, The Holder of the World.*
     Leave It To Me.
Iris Murdoch, *Under the Net.*
Vladimir Nabokov, *Lolita. Pale Fire.*
V. S. Naipaul, *A House for Mrs. Biswas. A Bend in the River.*
Flannery O'Connor, *Wise Blood. A Good Man is Hard to Find.*

The Violent Bear It Away.
Everything that Rise Must Converge.
John O'Hara, *Appointment in Samarra.*
Tillie Olsen, *Mother to Daughter, Daughter to Mother:*
Mothers on Mothering: A Day Book and Reader.
Silences. Tell Me a Riddle.
George Orwell, *1984. Animal Farm.*
John Dos Passos, *U.S.A.* (trilogy)
Alan Paton, *Cry the Beloved Country.*
Walker Percy, *The Moviegoer.*
Anthony Powell, *A Dance to the Music of Time.* (series)
Katherine Anne Porter, *Ship of Fools.*
Santha Rama Rau, *Gifts of Passage.*
Majorie Kinnan Rawlings, *Cross Creek.*
Jean Rhys, *Wide Saragasso Sea.*
Philip Roth, *Portnoy's Complaint .*
Salman Rushdie, *Midnight's Children.*
J. D. Salinger, *The Catcher in the Rye.*
Scott Russell Sanders, *Aurora Means Dawn.*
The Floating House.
George Santayana, *Soliloquies in England.*
Richard Seltzer, *The Name of Hero: A Novel.*
Leslie Marmon Silko, *Ceremony.*
Wallace Stegner, *Angle of Repose.*
John Steinbeck, *The Grapes of Wrath.*
William Styron, *Sophie's Choice.*
Amy Tan, *The Joy Luck Club.*
Booth Tarkington, *The Magnificent Amberson's.*
Paul Theroux, *The Blach House. Chicago Loop.*
The Family Arsenal. Girls at Play.
Half Moon Street. The Mosquito Coast.
Lionel Trilling, *The Liberal Imagination.*
Anne Tyler, *Dinner at the Homesick Restaurant.*
The Accidental Tourist. Breathing Lessons.
John Updike, *The Afterlife and Other Stories.*
Assorted Prose.
Kurt Vonnegut, *Slaughterhouse Five.*
Alice Walker, *The Color Purple.*
Robert Penn Warren, *All the King's Men.*
Evelyn Waugh, *A Handful of Dust. Scoop. Brideshead Revisited.*
Eudora Welty, Collection of Short Stories: *A Curtain of Green.*
The Wide Net. The Golden Apples.

Novels: *The Ponder Heart. Losing Battles.*
The Optimist's Daughter. One Writer's Beginnings.
Cornel West , *Jews and Blabks: Let the Hesaling Begin.*
Race Matters. Restoring Hope.
Nathaniel West, *The Day of the Locust.*
Edith Wharton, *The Age of Innocence. The House of Mirth.*
John Edgar Widemen, *Brothers and Keepers.*
Thornton Wilder, *The Bridge of San Luis Rey.*
Virginia Woolf, *To the Lighthouse.*
Thomas Wolfe, *Look Homeward Angel.*
Of Time and the River. The Web and the Rock
You Can't Go Home Again. The Hills Beyond
Virginia Woolf, *Moments of Being. A Writer's Diary.*
Mrs. Dalloway. The Common Reader.
To the Lighthouse. The Wave.

Chapter Two: The Essay Section-Literature and Composition AP

The Essay – Literature and Composition

Suggestions for Writing Any Timed Essay

1. Materials — On the day of the test, you will receive a green booklet with essay questions on three passages and a pink, six page, double-sided essay booklet to write your essays on the passages. You can mark up the green passage booklet and keep it at the end of the exam, but everything in the pink essay booklet will be turned in for a grade. With this in mind, have a good plan for writing before you make any entries in the pink booklet!

2. Prewriting — Most students want to begin writing too soon, and then rewrite the entire essay to make it neat. The end result is usually a neat, but rather shallow essay that results in boring reading and a failing grade. Correct this bad habit by practicing a close reading of each passage before actual writing begins.

3. Close Reading — Read the question and the passage a *first time* to understand the main focus of the passage (the author's or speaker's attitude, tone, point of view; OR the work's most significant literary element, meaning, or effect). Then read the question and the passage a *second time*, marking up the passage in the green booklet when you see connections between how the author manipulated the language to create his focus. Finally, read the passage a *third time* to look for hidden meanings that will help you form a meaningful thesis. Do this in the first 15 to 20 minutes. Do not begin writing in the pink booklet until you have read the passage three times!!!

3. Discovery through Writing — You have thought about the question enough now to begin properly. Write a strong opening sentence. Don't write flowery, general beginnings. Get right to the point. Rather than force the same five paragraph

model into every passage, use the organization of the passage as a model for the organization of your essay. Change your paragraph when the author changes views or explores a different shade of meaning, etc. Do not simply paraphrase the passage or discuss in general the use of particular literary or stylistic devices or catalogue various literary or stylistic elements in the passage without relating them to the author's intended or probable attitude, tone, point of view; OR the work's most significant literary element, meaning, or effect. Continue to discover as you write so you can reveal something about the passage in the end that is perceptive.

4. Quantity - The essay booklet you will receive has six double-sided pages. Each essay should be long enough to answer the question. An incomplete essay will get a low score. Think in terms of filling up the booklet. That's four pages per essay, written on both sides. Skipping one of the three essays will guarantee failure. Practice writing under timed conditions so you have "the feel" for a forty minute essay. Train yourself to stop at the end of forty minutes. Train yourself to have a completed essay at the end of forty minutes.

5. Quality — Quality is better than quantity. Good essays have the following three things in common. They:
       A. Answer all parts of the question fully;
       B. Support with unified, specific, adequate, accurate and representative evidence; and
       C. Are written maturely.

6. Make your handwriting as neat as possible. Use a ball point pen. Avoid felt tipped pens as they will bleed through the paper making it more difficult to read. Write on both sides of the paper. When you reread the essay at its completion and want to revise something, simply cross out the word or phrase with one line and insert the revision.

7. Practice Perfectly — Do as many essays in this Guide as possible under timed conditions, following the steps as outlined above. Overlearn the technique so the mechanics of *close reading* and *discovery through writing* become natural for you.

Good Luck ! ! !

The Essay – Literature and Composition

Typical Questions

The three forty minute essays on the Literature and Composition Exam usually follow a consistent pattern: one question on a passage of prose, one question on a poem, and one question on a work freely chosen by the student (usually called the "open" question). One variation may occur. Instead of writing on one passage or poem, the student may be asked to contrast two passages or two poems. Many of the passage analysis strategies used in the Language and Composition portion of the essay test can be applied to the prose and poetry questions of the Literature and Composition essay test with some modification. The free choice essay, however, emphasizes more of the literary aspects of literature.

Types of Prose Questions

The following is a composite of some of the prose questions asked since 1970. These prose questions can be divided into four different types of questions: Tone-Attitude-Point of View, Effect, Literary Elements, or Comparison and Contrast.

Applying these questions to any prose reading assigned can improve critical reading ability and increase chances of higher scores on the AP exam.

Tone — Attitude — Point of View: This type of question appeared 27 times in the last 29 years. In this essay the writer is asked to analyze how the author or character uses the language (presents the events in the story, or manipulates point of view) to establish the author or character's attitude (or feelings) toward someone or something. The question will ask you to address three to six stylistic and rhetorical devices (such as diction - syntax - tone - choice, selection and presentation of details, imagery, narrative structure) which are used by the author to convey that view.

Tone — Attitude — Point of View questions direct the student to show, explain or demonstrate how . . .

1. The character or narrator establishes his/her attitude toward the coming of a season.

2. The author's style reveals his/her feelings about the family he/she describes.

3. The writer establishes an attitude toward a family member's death. Using specific references to the text, show how the author's manipulation of language serves to convey his/her attitude.

4. The writer has an attitude toward ____ and therefore makes certain assumptions about human nature. Define precisely what that attitude and those assumptions are and analyze how the writer uses the language to convince the reader that his/her position is correct.

5. The author directs the reader's perceptions of the characters in the opening of a novel through his use of such stylistic devices as ___, ____, ____, and ___.

6. The author uses stylistic devices to convey his/her views on the concept of leisure which has lost its place in the society of his/her own time.

7. The author's use of techniques define ____'s character. Be sure to describe the author's attitude toward the ____.

8. The style and tone of the passage helps to express the author's attitudes.

9. Narrative techniques and other resources of language are used by the author to characterize ____ and ____'s attitude toward____.

10. The author conveys his view of ____ through the use of such elements as ____, ____, ____, and ____.

Effect: This type of question appeared four times since 1970 in the form of comparison/contrast questions, poetry passage analyses, or prose passage analyses. This type of question asks the writer to show how the effect of world and the way of life described (or the effect of the revisions made from an earlier draft, or the differing effects the writers want to have on the audience) is created by the writer's use of diction, syntax, imagery, tone, humor, pathos, and the grotesque.

Effect questions direct the student to show, explain or demonstrate how . . .

1. The world and the way of life described in the passage creates an overall effect.
2. The writer uses ____, ____, and ____ to produce an effect on the reader.
3. The blend of ___, ___, and ____ creates an effect.

The following language devices are named as suggestions for the writer to consider when analyzing how the author creates effect: diction - syntax - imagery - tone - humor - pathos and the grotesque.

Literary Elements: This question appeared seven times in the last 28 years. This type of the question asks the writer to describe the significance of a basic element of the work (plot, conflict, characterization, or setting) or define the attitude that the author would like the reader to adopt toward an element of the work. It also asks the writer to analyze how the author uses the resources of language (such as theme, symbol, setting, characterization, word choice or diction, imagery, phrasing, sentence structure, narrative pace, point of view, concrete language and structure) to achieve his/her purpose, or to promote that attitude.

Literary Elements (characterization, plot, setting, etc.) questions direct the student to show, explain or demonstrate how:

1. Two people are "naturally suited" for one another.
2. The author prepares the reader for the character's unwillingness or inability to act. Consider at least two elements of fiction such as ____, ____, ____, _____.

3. The order of events have significance.

4. The author's presentation of details is intended to shape the reader's attitudes toward the setting he describes. Give specific attention to the function of ____, ____, ____, ____.

5. This passage provides a characterization and evaluation of ____ more than of ____.

6. The author dramatizes ____'s adventure. Consider such elements as ____, ____, ____, ____.

7. The author uses literary techniques to characterize the main character .

The following literary techniques are named as suggestions for the writer to consider when analyzing how the author reveals a literary element of the story: theme - symbol - setting - image - characterization - word choice - imagery - phrasing - sentence structure - diction - imagery - narrative pace - point of view.

Comparison and Contrast: These type of questions seem to be one of the newest trends in testing for Language and Literature exams. Each year, both exams seem to be directing the student to perform some sort of comparison and contrast task . These type of questions ask the writer to analyze how such language devices as diction, sentence structure, presentation of details, revisions, imagery, movement of verse, form, and tone present different attitudes (different views of the nature of each speaker or writer, different assumptions, or different effects).

Comparison and Contrast questions direct the student to show, explain or demonstrate how:

1. The nature of each speaker, his assumptions about his audience, and the effects he wants to have on ____ differ in each passage. Consider the ___ and ___ of each passage.

2. Each author's ___ and ___ is intended to shape the reader's attitudes toward ____.

3. Two eye-witness accounts of ____s show different attitudes. Consider the different effects on the reader of the two accounts.

4. The writer makes revisions from the earlier to the later draft that change the effect of how the experience of ____ affected his attitude toward language. Discuss the probable reasons for the writer's additions and deletions and the ways in which

those revisions change the effect of the paragraph.

5. A writer shows the differences between the writing of two other authors. Analyze his attitude toward each writer and the devices he uses to convey those views.

The following devices are named as suggestions for the writer to consider when analyzing how the authors create different attitudes, effects, personalities, and/or assumptions: diction - sentence structure - presentation of details.

The Essay — Literature and Composition

Poetry Passage

The following is a composite of the types of poetry questions asked since 1970. These poetry questions can be divided into three different types of questions: Tone-Attitude-Point of View, Meaning, or Comparison and Contrast.

Applying these questions to any poetry reading assigned can improve your critical reading ability and increase your chance to score higher on the AP exam.

Tone —Attitude —Point of View: This type of question appeared 27 times in the last 29 years. In this essay the writer is asked to analyze how the poet or speaker uses the language (presents the events in the story, or manipulates point of view) to establish the poet's, or speaker's attitude (or feelings) toward someone or something. The question will ask you to address three to six stylistic and rhetorical devices (such as imagery - diction - verse form - language - devices of sound - allusions - syntax - tone., and other resources of language) which are used by the author to convey that view.

Tone — Attitude — Point of View questions direct the student to show, explain or demonstrate how:

1. The speaker's attitude toward a person is described in a poem.

2. The _____ of the last stanza of the poem is related to the speaker's earlier view of himself and his view of how others see him.

3. The poet's _____ reveals his attitude toward the two ways of _____ mentioned in the poem.

4. The speaker's attitude toward _____ in the last sestet is related to her attitude toward _____ in the first octave. Using specific references from the text, show how _____ and _____ contributes to the reader's understanding of these attitudes.

5. The language of the poem reflects the changing perceptions and emotions of the speaker toward _____. Develop your essay with specific references to the text of the poem.

6. The attitude of _____ and _____ are contrasted. Through careful analysis of _____ and _____, show how this contrast is important to the meaning of the poem.

7. The language of the poem reflects both the neighbor's and the narrator's perception _____. Discuss how the portrayal of _____ is enhanced by such features as _____, _____ and _____.

8. The _____, _____ and _____ of the soliloquy from _____ conveys the King's state of mind.

9. The poet's use of language reveals the speaker's attitude toward the woman's death.

10. The poem's _____, _____ and _____ trace the speaker's changing responses to encountering unfamiliar aspects of the natural world.

11. The speaker uses the various _____ of the poem to reveal his attitude toward the nature of _____.

Meaning: This question appeared five times on the poetry exam since 1970. This type of question asks the writer to define how conceptions differ from one stanza to another, or to reveal literal and figurative meanings, or to prepare the reader for the final response. This type of question also asks the writer to show how these meanings relate to the title, or are created by such things as organization of the poem, use of concrete details, diction, figurative language, imagery, language, structure, or point of view.

Meaning questions direct the student to show, explain or demonstrate how:

1. The conceptions of _____ in lines 1-34 differ than those in lines 35-60.

2. The _____ and _____ reveal both its literal and figurative meanings. In your discussion, show how both these meanings relate to the title.

3. The poem's _____, _____, and _____ prepare the reader for the final response.

4. _____, _____, _____ convey meaning in the poem .

Comparison and Contrast: These type of questions seem to be one of the newest trends in testing for Language and Literature exams. Each year, both exams seem to be directing the student to perform some sort of comparison and contrast task . These type of questions ask the writer to analyze how such language devices as diction, sentence structure, presentation of details, revisions, imagery, movement of verse, form, and tone present different attitudes (different views of the nature of each speaker or writer, different assumptions, or different effects).

Comparison and Contrast questions direct the student to show, explain or demonstrate how:. .

1. The characteristics of the second poem make it better than the first poem. Refer specifically to the details of both poems.

2. The attitudes toward the coming of a season implied in these two poems differ from each other. Refer specifically to the texts.

3. The two poems presenting encounters with____ have different attitudes (toward nature, toward the solitary individual, etc.). Distinguish between the attitudes expressed in the poems and discuss the techniques that the poets use to present the attitudes.

4. The ____, ____, and ____ of the verse in the two major sections of the same poem are different in tone and content.

5. The following two poems have similarities and differences. Consider ____ and ____ when analyzing these differences.

6. The ____, ____, ____, and ____ contrast the speakers' different views of ____ in the two poems.

The Essay - Literature and Composition

Writing Comparison/ Contrast Questions

Find passages that have differing views on a similar subject. Then use the following questions to write a comparison and contrast essay about the two works or two passages:

1. In the following two passages, both author's seem to portray their character as ____. In a well-organized essay, analyze how each author uses imagery, diction, and descriptive language to illustrate different aspects of ____.

2. The speaker in both passages below is describing a ____. After reading both passages, analyze how each author uses language differently to portray the speaker's attitude toward his/her ____.

3. The following passages show characters who have contrasting views of ____. Read these passages, then show how each author uses vivid details, selective diction, and similes to portray the different views.

4. The following two poems discuss the importance of ____. Read the poems. Then write an essay demonstrating how this importance is displayed differently through the use of diction, imagery, and sound devices.

5. In the following passages, each character is running away from ____. Read the passages carefully. Then write a well-organized essay in which you describe the author's attitude toward how the character deals with his/her ____.
6. Discuss ____ as a recurring motif in each of the passages. Analyze how the language affects the character's attitude.

7. The passages below deal with less than average ____ role models. How do the similar language devices displayed reveal different aspects of each character's disgrace?

8. In the passages below, each character is displaying despicable behavior. Analyze how each author uses similar rhetorical and stylistic devices to reveal different levels of disapproval toward these character's actions.

9. The characters in the following passages are involved in similar conflicts. How does each author use such devices as imagery, descriptive diction, and allusions to make the conflicts seem real to the reader?

10. The passages below deal with two villains (or heroes). After reading each passage carefully, write an essay in which you analyze how each narrator presents these villains (or heroes). Consider such rhetorical features as tone, imagery, and effect.

11. In the following passages, both characters are being judged by a(an) ____ on the subject of ____. Read the passages carefully. Then write a well-organized essay describing how each author uses literary devices to portray the _____' attitudes toward ____.

12. In the following poems, both characters show a change in attitude. After carefully reading these passages, analyze the language devices used to illustrate this change.

The Open Question

Since the free choice asks the writer to select a distinguished novel or play to use as evidence to answer the question, students need to preview previously read literature in terms of its literary merit in case this literature may be appropriate to use. Extensive reading from the list of suggested authors on pp. 2 - 10 of *A Practical Guide to the AP English Literature and Composition Examination* is also recommended. I have divided these free-choice (open) questions into the basic elements of fiction: plot/conflict, setting, characterization, narration, theme, and style. Many are followed by quotes from works of literary merit that show some application for the question.

Applying these questions to the reading of any novel or play assigned can improve your critical thinking skills and increase your chance to score higher on the AP exam.

Plot/Conflict: In a selected work of literary merit, show, explain or demonstrate how . . .

1. The author reveals a character's unwillingness or inability to act through such elements of fiction as theme, symbol, setting, image, characterization, or other aspects of the narrative artist's craft.

    A. *A Woman of No Importance* by Oscar Wilde: "She loved him — before the child was born — for she had a child. She implored him for the child's sake to marry her, that the child might have a name, that her sin might not be visited on the child, who was innocent. He refused."

    B. *Mansfield Park* by Jane Austen: "She had more fears of her perseverance to remove . . . ill-nature — selfishness — and a fear of exposing herself"

    C. *The Old Man and the Sea* by Ernest Hemingway:

    D. *For Whom the Bell Tolls* by Ernest Hemingway:

    E. *Lucy Gayheart* by Willa Cather:

    F?

2. Any implausible or strikingly unrealistic incident or character, if evident, is related to the more realistic or plausible elements in the rest of the work.

> A. *The Scarlet Letter* by Nathaniel Hawthorne: "Not a stitch in that embroidered letter, but she had felt in her heart."
>
> C. *Maggie: A Girl of the Streets* by Stephen Crane: "The girl, Maggie, blossomed in a mud puddle. She grew to be a most rare and wonderful production of the tenement district, a pretty girl. None of the dirt of Rum Alley seemed to be in her veins. The philosophers upstairs, downstairs and on the same floor, puzzled over it."
>
> D. *Things Fall Apart* by Chinua Achebe: "Every clan and village had its evil forest. In it were buried all those who died of the really evil diseases, like leprosy and smallpox. It was also the dumping ground for potent fetishes of great medicine men when they died. An evil forest was, therefore, alive with sinister forces and powers of darkness."
>
> E. *A Tale of Two Cities* by Charles Dickens: "Twas a blank and bleary, yet most frivolous night, when we first began our venture down Dead Man's Path through the heart of evil. Suddenly a wretched voice set out of the hills and raised the hair on our bodies. So horrible was the sound that many ran away in fear of being eaten."
>
> F. *My Antonia* by Willa Cather
>
> G?

3. Some works create a significant conflict between a parent (or a parent figure) and a son or daughter. Analyze the sources of the conflict and explain how the conflict contributes to the meaning of the work.

> A. *Washington Square* by Henry James: "I want to marry Morris, but if I do, it will disappoint my father greatly."
>
> B. *Maggie: A Girl of the Streets* by Stephen Crane: "Here, you Jim, git up, now, while I belt yer life out, you damned disorderly brat."

C. *Things Fall Apart* by Chinua Achebe: "Okonkwo did not have the start in life which many young men usually had. He did not inherit a barn from his father. There was no barn to inherit."

D. *The Color Purple* by Alice Walker:

E?

4. Writers who get the best response are writers who offer a happy ending through moral development . . . some kind of spiritual reassessment or moral reconciliation, even with the self, even at death.

A. *The Adventures of Huckleberry Finn* by Mark Twain

B. *The Color Purple* by Alice Walker

C. *Crime and Punishment* by Dostoevsky

D. *Great Expectations* by Charles Dickens

E. *A Doll's House* by Ibsen

Setting: In a selected work of literary merit, show, explain or demonstrate how . . .

5. Some moments or scenes are especially memorable. Select a line or so of poetry, or a moment or scene in a novel or play that you find especially memorable. Identify the line of passage; explain its relationship to the work in which it is found; and analyze the reason for its effectiveness.

A. *The Secret Agent* by Joseph Conrad: "Before reaching Knightsbridge, Mr. Verloc took a turn to the left out of the busy main thorouhfare, uproarious with the traffic of omnibuses and trotting vans, into the almost silent, swift flow of hansoms."

B. *Maggie: A Girl of the Streets* by Stephen Crane: "Long streamers of garments fluttered from fire escapes. In all unhandy places there were buckets, brooms, rags, and bottles. In the street infants played or fought with other infants or sat stupidly in the way of vehicles. Formidable woman, with uncombed hair and disordered dress, gossiped while leaning on railings, or screamed in frantic quarrels. Withered persons, in curious postures of submission to something, sat smoking pipes in obscure corners. A thousand odors of cooking food came forth to the street. The building quivered and creaked from the weight of humanity stamping about in its bowels."

C. *A Tale of Two Cities* by Charles Dickens: "It was the best of times, it was the worst of times, it was the age of wisdom, it was the age of foolishness, it was the epoch of belief, it was the epic of incredulity, it was the season of light, it was the season of darkness, it was the spring of hope, it was the winter of despair, we had everything before us, we had nothing before us, we were all going to heaven, we were all going the other way . . . ."

D. *For Whom the bell Tolls* by Ernest Hemingway

E. *The Old Man and the Sea* by Ernest Hemingway

F?

6. Many plays and novels use contrasting places (for example, two countries, two cities or towns, two houses, or the land and the sea) to represent opposed forces or ideas which are central to the meaning of the work. Select a work of literary merit that contrasts two places, explaining how the places differ, what each place represents, and how their contrasts contribute to the meaning of the work.

A. *A Woman of No Importance* by Oscar Wilde: "We have the largest country in the world, Lady Caroline. They used to tell us at school that some of our states are as big as France and England put together."

B. *Lucy Gayheart* by Willa Cather

C. *The Color Purple* by Alice Walker

D?

Characterization: In a selected work of literary merit, show, explain or demonstrate how . . .

7. Two characters are portrayed as being naturally or unnaturally suited for one another.

A. *The Turn of the Screw* by Henry James: "He knew me as well as I knew him; and so, in the cold, faint twilight, with a glimmer in the high glass and another on the polish of the oak stair below, we faced each other in our common intensity."

B. *The Bellarosa Connection* by Saul Bellow

C. *My Antonia* by Willa Cather

D?

8. Characters are always portrayed as being affected by and responding to the standards of a society. Describe the standards of the society in which the character exists, and show how the character is affected by and responds to the standards.

A. *A Woman of No Importance* by Oscar Wilde: "Well, you couldn't come to a more charming place than this, Miss Worsley, though the house is excessively damp, unpardonably damp, and dear Lady Hunstanton is sometimes a little lax about the people she asks down here."

B. *The House of Seven Gables* by Nathaniel Hawthorne: "Her new experience has led our decayed gentlewoman to very disagreeable conclusions as to the temper and manners of what was termed the lower class, whom heretofore she had looked down upon with a gentle and pitying complaisance, as herself occupying a sphere of unquestionable superiority."

C. *The Color Purple* by Alice Walker

D?

9. The stereotyped character is employed successfully to achieve the author's purpose.

A. *Tar Baby* by Toni Morrison:

B. *The Adventures of Huckleberry Finn* by Mark Twain

C. *A Doll's House* by Ibsen

D. *A Street Car Named Desire* by Tennessee Williams

E?

10. The full presentation of a complex character in the work, whose actions alone define him as evil or immoral, makes us react more sympathetically than we otherwise might. This villain, also, always enhances the meaning of the work.

> A. *The Secret Agent* by Joseph Conrad: Mr. Verloc: "I don't want to look at you as long as I live."
> B. *The Grapes of Wrath* by John Steinbeck
> C. *The Adventures of Huckleberry Finn* by Mark Twain
> D?

11. One of the characters is always a confidant (male) or confidante (female), often a friend or relative of the hero or heroine, whose role is to be present when the hero or heroine needs a sympathetic listener to confide in. However, the author sometimes uses this character for other purposes as well. Choose a confidant or confidante from a novel or play and discuss the various ways this character functions in the work.

> A. *Washington Square* by Henry James
> B. *The Adventures of Huckleberry Finn*
> by Mark Twain
> C. *The Great Gatsby* by F. Scot Fitzgerald

12. A character who appears briefly, or does not appear at all, is a significant presence who affects action, theme, or the development of other characters.

> A. *Maggie: A Girl of the Streets* by Stephen Crane: "The babe, Tommy, died. He went away in a white, insignificant coffin, his small waxen hand clutching a flower that the girl, Maggie, had stolen from an Italian."
> B?

13. Writers often highlight the values of a culture or a society by using characters who are alienated from that culture or society because of gender, race, class or creed. This alienation always reveals something about the surrounding society's assumptions and moral values.

> A. *The Scarlet Letter* by Nathaniel Hawthorne:
> "Hester set forth to the place appointed for her punishment (a scaffold). This scaffold constituted a portion of a penal machine which . . . was held, in the old time, to be as effectual an agent, in the promotion of good citizenship, as ever was the guillotine among the terrorists of France. It was, in short, the platform of the pillory; and above it rose the framework of that instrument of discipline, so fashioned as to confine the human head in its tight grasp, and thus holding it up to the public gaze. The very ideal of ignominy was embodied and made manifest in this contrivance of wood and iron."
> B?

Narration: In a selected work of literary merit, show, explain or demonstrate how . . .

14. The element of time is used in a distinct way. The chronological sequence of events may be altered, or time may be suspended or altered . . . contributing to the effectiveness of the work as a whole.

> A. *The Turn of the Screw* by Henry James: "At this point I precipitately found myself aware of three things. They were practically simultaneous, yet they had flashes of succession."
> B. *Lucy Gayheart* by Willa Cather: (The entire novel is a flashback.)
> C. *My Antonia* by Willa Cather
> D?

15. Some of the most significant events are always mental or psychological; for example, awakenings, discoveries or changes in consciousness. Describe how the author of a work of literary merit gives these internal events the sense of excitement, suspense, and climax usually associated with external action.

A. *The Secret Agent* by Joseph Conrad: "The prospect of having to break the news to her had put him in a fever. Chief Inspector Heat had relieved him of that task. . . . . It remained now for him to face her grief."
B. *The Old man and the Sea* by Ernest Hemingway:
C?

Theme: In a selected work of literary merit, show, explain or demonstrate how . . .

16. Limitations of some aspect of contemporary society are reflected in a selected work of literary merit.
A. *A Woman of No Importance* by Oscar Wilde: "Only two kinds of society: the plain and the colored."
B?

17. The opening scene of a drama or the first chapter of a novel introduces some of the major themes of the work.
A. *The Old man and the Sea* by Ernest Hemingway
B. *The Scarlet Letter* by Nathaniel Hawthorne: "Before this ugly edifice, and between it and the wheel track of the street, was a grass plot, much overgrown with burdock, pigweed, appleperu, and such unsightly vegetation, which evidently found something congenial in the soil that had so early borne the black flower of civilized society, a prison."
C?

18. A selected work of literary merit, although written before 1900, has relevance for a person today.
A?
B?

19. A character exists who has a misconception of himself or his world. Show how destroying or perpetuating this illusion contributes to the central theme of the play.
A?
B?

20. The conflict created when the will of an individual op-
poses the will of the majority is a recurring theme. Analyze
the conflict seen in your work and discuss the moral and ethi-
cal implications for both the individual and society.

     A?

     B?

21. A character's attempt to recapture or reject the past is an
important theme in many plays, novels, and poems. Choose
a work in which a character views the past with such feelings
as reverence, bitterness, or longing. Show with clear evidence
how the character's view of the past is used to develop a theme
in the work.

     A. *The Secret Agent* by Joseph Conrad: "You'll have
to pull yourself together, my girl," he said, sympathetically. "What's done can't be undone."

     B. *My Antonia* by Willa Cather

22. A recurring theme may also be the classic war between
passion and responsibility.   For instance, a personal cause, a
love, a desire for revenge, a determination to redress a wrong,
or some other emotion or drive that conflicts with moral duty.
Choose a literary work in which the character confronts the
demands of a private passion that conflicts with his/her re-
sponsibilities. Show clearly the nature of the conflict, its effect
upon the character, and the significance to the work.

     A. *For Whom the Bell Tolls* by Ernest Hemingway

     B. *Tar Baby* by Toni Morrison

23. Some works of literary merit seem to advocate changes in
social or political attitudes or in traditions. Choose a novel or
play and note briefly the particular attitudes or traditions that
the author apparently wishes to modify. Then analyze the techniques the author uses to influence the reader's or audience's
views.

     A?

     B?

Style: In a selected work of literary merit, show, explain or demonstrate how . . .

24. The title has significance that is developed through the author's use of devices such as contrast, repetition, allusion, and point of view.

> A. *The Secret Agent* by Joseph Conrad: "Night, the inevitable reward of man's faithful labors on this earth, night had fallen on Mr. Verloc, the tired revolutionist — 'one of the old lot' — the humble guardian of society; the invaluable **secret agent** . . . a servant of law and order, faithful, trusted, accurate, admirable, with perhaps one single amiable weakness: the idealistic belief of being loved for himself."
>
> B?

25. Each author's presentation of details (word choice, imagery, phrasing, and sentence structure) is intended to shape the reader's attitudes toward the place or person he describes.

> A. *A Woman of No Importance* by Oscar Wilde: "To get into the best society, nowadays, one either has to feed people, amuse people, or shock people — that is all."
>
> B. *The Turn of the Screw* by Henry James: "My candle, under a bold flourish, went out, and I perceived, by the uncovered window, that the yielding dusk of earliest morning rendered it unnecessary."
>
> C. *The Scarlet Letter* by Nathaniel Hawthorne: "Stretching forth the official staff in his left hand, he laid his right upon the shoulder of a woman, whom he thus drew forward; until, on the threshold of the prison door, she repelled him by an action marked with natural dignity and force of character, and stepped into the open air, as if by her own free will."
>
> D?

26. The ending appropriately or inappropriately concludes the work.

> A. *The House of Seven Gables* by Nathaniel Hawthorne: "Maules Well, all this time, though left in solitude, was throwing up a succession of kaleidoscopic pictures in which a gifted eye might have foreshadowed

the coming fortunes of . . . ."
B?

27. The meaning of some literary works is often enhanced by sustained allusions to myths, the Bible, or other works of literature. Select a literary work that makes use of a sustained reference. Explain the allusion that predominates the work and analyze how it enhances the work's meaning.
   A. *Tar Baby* by Toni Morrison
   B?

28. The audience is confronted with a scene or scenes of violence which contribute to the meaning of the complete work.
   A. *Native Son* by Richard Wright
   B. *Maggie: A Girl of the Streets* by Stephen Crane
   C?

29. One important measure of a superior work of literature is its ability to produce in the reader a healthy confusion of pleasure and disquietude. Select a work that produces this healthy confusion. Explain the sources of the pleasure and disquietude experienced by the reader of the work.
   A?
   B?

30. Some works have a blend of humor, pathos, and the grotesque.
   A. *Maggie: A Girl of the Streets* by Stephen Crane:
   "Once, when a lady had dropped her purse on the sidewalk, the gnarled and leathery woman had grabbed it and smuggled it with great dexterity beneath her cloak. When she was arrested she cursed the lady in a partial swoon, and with her aged limbs, twisted from rheumatism, had almost kicked the stomach out of a huge policeman whose conduct she referred to when she said: "The police, damn 'em."
   B?
   C?

31. Some works make a good case for distortion as a way of making people see.

> A. *The Scarlet Letter* by Nathaniel Hawthorne: The Scarlet Letter "had the effect of a spell, taking her out of the ordinary relations with humanity, and enclosing her in a sphere within herself."
>
> B?

32. Sometimes a scene or character awakens "thoughtful laughter" in the reader.

> A?
>
> B?

The Essay –

Student Grading Made Easy With Comprehensive Checklists:

Each essay question written by Advanced Placement personnel is graded by a set of Rubrics. Sample Rubrics are available through *The Advanced Placement Program: The College Board*. Examining these Rubrics, I discovered that they addressed nine separate categories. Designing a checklist with nine items to arrive at a score from one to nine is a result of this discovery. I use the checklists in the following ways.

New Learning: These checklists are designed to help students understand what is expected by AP for each type of question. When introducing a new type of essay, I refer them to the appropriate checklist on pages 40 - 51 and discuss its content. This prepares them for effective writing by making them familiar with the AP expectations for that particular essay. I then have them apply those checklists to writing an AP essay on that type of question. Becoming familiar with what is expected by AP for each type of question helps the student read more critically and write more maturely.

Student Grading: These checklists are also designed to help students grade each other's essays. These checklists make the grading as objective and easy as possible. After completing any practice essay assigned, I usually have students from a different AP section grade these anonymously using the checklist that would apply to that question. They do this by filling out a generic cover sheet using the proper checklist in this chapter as a guide. This provides student feedback that can be used in conferencing (See "Checklist Cover Sheet" on next page).

Multiple Conferencing: Perhaps the best feature of the checklists is that they demand dialogue among the learners. I grade the essays holistically, placing a pencilled mark from one to nine in my grade book. If my mark varies more than two points from the combined results of the two graders, I confer with them. Once students get their results back, they are required to record their grades with me. Here they are allowed to negotiate for a higher grade if they can adequately defend their writing. Students improve their own writing through this type of multiple-conferencing system more quickly than through any other system I've used.

Reinforced Learning: The checklists can also be used as a question recognition check. Once all the types of questions are taught in steps one through three, we still read continuously. Occasionally, I will write an AP question on the board that addresses this reading. Then I have them write the essay in one class period. At the end of the period they receive a "Checklist Cover Sheet." Placing the correct name of the type of essay on the top, they turn this in with their essay when it is ready to grade. Picking the right checklist from pages 40 - 51 helps them recognize the requirements of the question. For instance, if they define the meaning of the passage instead of the speaker's attitude, they have not answered the question, and even though their essay may be maturely written, they will receive a low score because they did not answer the question.

Use the Checklist Cover Sheet on the next two pages in conjunction with the complete checklists that follow.

The Essay Checklist

Student Writer Name   -   Class Period

Type of Essay

from _____
(Author - *Title*)

STEP 1: Check each item listed below which accurately describes the positive aspects of the essay being graded. Add one point for each item checked from the list. This side describes the basic requirements for a well-written essay. (Grader one should check column one. Grader two should check column two):

___-___1.   GRADER RESPONSE:

___-___2.

___-___3.

___-___4.

___-___5.

___-___6.

___-___7.

___-___8.

___-___9.

MAXIMUM SCORE RESULTS: Grader 1 _____

MAXIMUM SCORE RESULTS: Grader 2 _____

STEP 2: Check each item which accurately describes the negative aspects of the essay being graded. This side describes how the essay may not be as good as the higher-scoring essays. (Grader one should check column one. Grader two should check column two):

___-___1.   GRADER RESPONSE:

___-___2.

___-___3.

___-___4.

___-___5.

___-___6.

___-___7.

___-___8.

___-___9.

RESULTS:

Grader 1: _____ - _____ = _____
        Step 1 Score   Step 2 Score

Grader 2: _____ - _____ = _____
        Step 1 Score   Step 2 Score

Grader 1 Score + Grader 2 Score = _____

Above sum
divided by 2 =

Score for essay

The Essay— Checklist for
Tone, POV, or Attitude

STEP 1: Check each item listed below which accurately describes the positive aspects of the essay being graded. Add one point for each item checked from the list. This side describes the basic requirements for a well-written essay. (Grader one should check column one. Grader two should check column two):

___-___1. The essay demonstrates an understanding of the author's (speaker's or character's) complex attitude.

___-___2. The essay analyzes how literary, stylistic, or narrative devices listed in the question or used in the passage or poem distinguish the complexity of the author's (speaker's or character's) attitude.

___-___3. The essay offers a convincing interpretation of the passage or poem.
.

___-___4. The writer's use of quotes shows an appreciation of the author's (poet's) style.

___-___5. The writer's explanations of the evidence are clear, concise and consistent with the meaning of the passage.

___-___6. This essay supports the discussion of each language device with apt and specific references to the text.

___-___7. The diction and sentence structure of this essay communicate a clear message.

___-___8. The implicit organization of this essay aids in communicating a clear message.

___-___9. The grammar aids in communicating a clear message.

MAXIMUM SCORE RESULTS: Grader 1 _____
MAXIMUM SCORE RESULTS: Grader 2 _____

STEP 2:   Check each item below which accurately describes the negative aspects of the essay being graded. This side describes how the essay may not be as good as the higher-scoring essays. (Grader one should check column one. Grader two should check column two):

___-___1. The essay's discussion of the author's (speaker's or character's) complex view is less incisive than those of the highest scoring essays.

___-___2. The writer discusses the literary, stylistic, or narrative devices with limited purpose or accuracy.

___-___3. The essay's interpretation of the passage or poem may be vague or pedestrian or incorrect.

___-___4. The writer's use of quotes is awkward, inappropriate, or uninteresting.

___-___5. The writer simply catalogues the rhetorical or stylistic devices without relating them to the creation of the author's (Speaker's or character's) attitude.

___-___6. Although adequate in quantity, the evidence in this essay is not as thorough or precise as the top-scoring essays.

___-___7. Distracting errors in diction or syntax make the message unclear.

___-___8. The organization of this essay is less appropriate than those of the top-scoring essays.

___-___9. The essay reveals consistent weakness in grammar and/or other basic elements of composition.

RESULTS:

Grader 1: _____ - _____ = _____
          Step 1 Score   Step 2 Score

Grader 2: _____ - _____ = _____
          Step 1 Score   Step 2 Score

Grader 1 Score + Grader 2 Score = _____

Above sum divided by 2 =

Score for essay

The Essay— Checklist for Effect

STEP 1: Check each item listed below which accurately describes the positive aspects of the essay being graded. Add one point for each item checked from the list. This side describes the basic requirements for a well-written essay. (Grader one should check column one. Grader two should check column two):

___-___1. The essay comments on the probable or intended effect of the passage with psychological insight.

___-___2. The essay analyzes how all the literary, narrative, or stylistic devices listed in the question or used in the passage define the author's probable or intended effect.

___-___3. The essay shows an excellent appreciation of the contextual relationships of the passage.

___-___4. The essay is written in an appropriate and interesting format.

___-___5. The thesis clearly shows the connection between the author's probable or intended effect and the language devices used to create that effect.

___-___6. The essay persuasively substantiates the discussion of each language device with a minimum of three embedded bits of quotes per paragraph.

___-___7. The diction and sentence structure of this essay communicate an understandable message.

___-___8. The ideas in this essay are expressed in an ordered or logical sequence.

___-___9. The grammar aids in communicating a clear message.

MAXIMUM SCORE RESULTS: Grader 1 _____

MAXIMUM SCORE RESULTS: Grader 2 _____

STEP 2:   Check each item below which accurately describes the negative aspects of the essay being graded. This side describes how the essay may not be as good as the higher-scoring essays. (Grader one should check column one. Grader two should check column two):

___-___1. The writer comments on the intended or probable effects in ways not supported by the text.

___-___2. The writer discusses the rhetorical and stylistic strategies with limited purpose or accuracy.

___-___3. The writer simply paraphrases the content of the passage.

___-___4. The writer simply catalogues the rhetorical or stylistic devices without relating them to the creation of the author's effect.

___-___5. The connection between the evidence and the author's purpose is less clear than those of the top-scoring essays.

___-___6. Although adequate in quantity, the evidence in this essay is not as convincing as the top-scoring essay.

___-___7. A few lapses in diction or syntax may be present, but the message is clear.

___-___8. The organization of this essay is less appropriate than those of the top-scoring essays.

___-___9. The essay reveals consistent weakness in grammar and/or other basic elements of composition.

RESULTS:

Grader 1: _____ - _____ = _____
                 Step 1 Score   Step 2 Score
Grader 2: _____ - _____ = _____
                 Step 1 Score   Step 2 Score
Grader 1 Score + Grader 2 Score = _____

Above sum divided by 2 =

Score for essay

The Essay—Checklist for Literary Elements

STEP 1: Check each item listed below which accurately describes the positive aspects of the essay being graded. Add one point for each item checked from the list. This side describes the basic requirements for a well-written essay. (Grader one should check column one. Grader two should check column two):

___-___1. The essay demonstrates an understanding of how the author reveals character, plot/conflict, setting, or theme.

___-___2. The essay analyzes how all the literary, narrative, or stylistic devices listed in the question or used in the passage capture the intensity of the character, plot/conflict, setting, or theme.

___-___3. The essay recognizes the complexity of the author's characterization, plot/conflict, setting, or theme.

___-___4. The essay presents an individual understanding of the text.

___-___5. The thesis clearly shows the connection between the author's language and the creation of character, plot/conflict, setting, or theme.

___-___6. The essay persuasively substantiates the discussion of each language device with a minimum of three embedded quotes per paragraph.

___-___7. The diction and sentence structure of this essay communicate an understandable message.

___-___8. The ideas in this essay are expressed in an ordered or logical sequence.

___-___9. The grammar aids in communicating a clear message.

MAXIMUM SCORE RESULTS: Grader 1 _____

MAXIMUM SCORE RESULTS: Grader 2 _____

STEP 2:   Check each item below which accurately describes the negative aspects of the essay being graded. This side describes how the essay may not be as good as the higher-scoring essays. (Grader one should check column one. Grader two should check column two):

___-___1. These writer's understanding of how the author reveals character, plot/conflict, setting, or theme is vague, mechanical, or overly generalized.

___-___2. The writer discusses the literary and stylistic strategies with limited purpose or accuracy.

___-___3. The writer simply paraphrases the content of the passage or says nothing beyond the easy and obvious to grasp.

___-___4. The essay reflects an incomplete understanding of the story and fails to respond adequately to the question.

___-___5. The discussion of how the author uses the language is misguided, inaccurate, or unclear.

___-___6. Although adequate in number, the evidence in this essay is not as convincing as the top-scoring essay.

___-___7. A few lapses in diction or syntax may be present, but the message is clear.

___-___8. The organization of this essay is less appropriate than those of the top-scoring essays.

___-___9. The essay reveals consistent weakness in grammar and/or other basic elements of composition.

RESULTS:

Grader 1: _____ - _____ = _____
Step 1 Score   Step 2 Score

Grader 2: _____ - _____ = _____
Step 1 Score   Step 2 Score

Grader 1 Score + Grader 2 Score = _____

Above sum divided by 2 =

Score for essay

The Essay—Checklist for Comparison and Contrast Essay

STEP 1: Check each item listed below which accurately describes the positive aspects of the essay being graded. Add one point for each item checked from the list. This side describes the basic requirements for a well-written essay. (Grader one should check column one. Grader two should check column two):

___-___1. The attitude, effect, or meaning defined demonstrates a perceptive insight into each of the works.

___-___2. The essay shows how all of the literary or stylistic devices seen in both passages are used differently to create an attitude, effect, or meaning.

___-___3. This writer has reached valid, pertinent, and relevant conclusions about the comparison.

___-___4. This writer has shown an appreciation of the contextual relationship between the two excerpts.

___-___5. The thesis clearly shows the connection between the author's (or poet's) attitude, effect, or meaning and the language devices used to convey that attitude.

___-___6. This essay supports the discussion of each language device with good and persuasive substantiation of both works (a minimum of three embedded quotes per paragraph).

___-___7. The diction and sentence structure of this essay communicate a clear message.

___-___8. The organization of this essay aids in communicating a clear message.

___-___9. The grammar aids in communicating a clear message.

MAXIMUM SCORE RESULTS: Grader 1 _____

MAXIMUM SCORE RESULTS: Grader 2 _____

STEP 2: Check each item below which accurately describes the negative aspects of the essay being graded. This side describes how the essay may not be as good as the higher-scoring essays. (Grader one should check column one. Grader two should check column two):

___-___1. The writer simply names the probable or intended attitude, effect, or meaning (or the three devices, or both) with no discussion.

___-___2. The writer discusses the literary and stylistic strategies with limited purpose or accuracy.

___-___3. The writer simply paraphrases each passage.

___-___4. The writer simply catalogues the rhetorical or stylistic devices without relating them to the creation of the authors' probable or intended attitude, effect, or meaning .

___-___5. The connection between the evidence and the authors' probable or intended attitude, effect, or meaning is less clear than those of the top-scoring essays.

___-___6. Although adequate in number, the evidence in this essay is not as convincing as the top-scoring essay.

___-___7. A few lapses in grammar, diction, or syntax may be present, but the message is clear.

___-___8. The organization of this essay is less appropriate than those of the top-scoring essays.

___-___9. The essay reveals consistent weakness in grammar and/or other basic elements of composition.

RESULTS:

Grader 1: _____ - _____ = _____
             Step 1 Score   Step 2 Score

Grader 2: _____ - _____ = _____
             Step 1 Score   Step 2 Score

Grader 1 Score + Grader 2 Score = _____

Above sum divided by 2 =

Score for essay

The Essay—Checklist
for Essays on Meaning

STEP 1:   Check each item listed below which accurately describes the positive aspects of the essay being graded. Add one point for each item checked from the list. This side describes the basic requirements for a well-written essay. (Grader one should check column one. Grader two should check column two):

___-___1. The essay clearly demonstrates an understanding of the poem's (passage's) literal and figurative meanings.

___-___2. The essay discusses how the language, structure, and imagery of the poem (or passage) are used to convey meaning.

___-___3. The essay supports the discussion of each language device with apt and specific evidence.

___-___4. The writer recognizes the multiple perspectives seen in the poem (or passage).

___-___5. The essay offers a convincing interpretation of the poem (or passage).

___-___6. The writer demonstrates an ability to read perceptively by saying something beyond the easy and obvious to grasp.

___-___7. The diction and sentence structure of this essay communicate a clear message.

___-___8. The organization of this essay aids in communicating a clear message.

___-___9. The grammar aids in communicating a clear message.

MAXIMUM SCORE RESULTS: Grader 1 _____
MAXIMUM SCORE RESULTS: Grader 2 _____

STEP 2:   Check each item below which accurately describes the negative aspects of the essay being graded. This side describes how the essay may not be as good as the higher-scoring essays. (Grader one should check column one. Grader two should check column two):

___-___1. The essay's definition of the poem's (passage's) meaning is less thorough or less precise than those of the highest-scoring essays .

___-___2. The essay's discussion of language, structure, and imagery is briefer and less incisive than those of the highest-scoring essays.

___-___3. The essay's discussion of language, structure, and imagery is less well-developed than the best papers.

___-___4. The writer misses the complexity of meaning that the poem (or passage) describes.

___-___5. The essay fails to respond to part(s) of the question.

___-___6. The discussion of meaning may be pedestrian, inaccurate, or unclear.

___-___7. A few lapses in diction or syntax may be present, but the message is clear.

___-___8. The organization of this essay is less appropriate than those of the top-scoring essays.

___-___9. The essay reveals consistent weakness in grammar and/or other basic elements of composition.

RESULTS:

Grader 1: _____ - _____ = _____

               Step 1 Score   Step 2 Score

Grader 2: _____ - _____ = _____

               Step 1 Score   Step 2 Score

Grader 1 Score + Grader 2 Score = _____

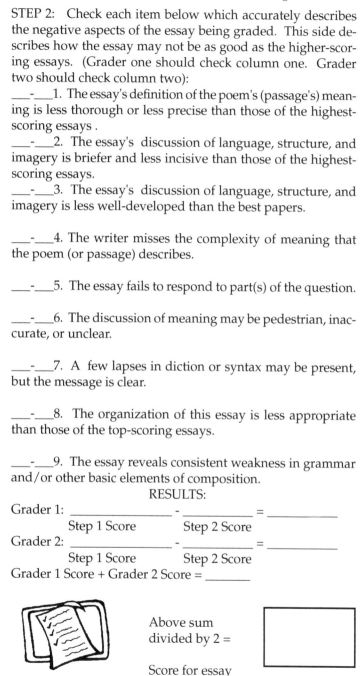

Above sum
divided by 2 =

Score for essay

The Essay—Checklist
for the "Open"
or "Free-Choice" Essay

STEP 1:   Check each item listed below which accurately describes the positive aspects of the essay being graded. Add one point for each item checked from the list. This side describes the basic requirements for a well-written essay. (Grader one should check column one. Grader two should check column two):

___-___1. The writer selects a suitable novel or play in which the literary element addressed in the question is significant to the work as a whole.

___-___2. The writer presents a reasonable explanation of the purpose and meaning of the work.

___-___3. The writer effectively establishes how the literary element addressed in the question is significant to the work as a whole.

___-___4. The writer effectively explains how the literary element is significant to the work as a whole.

___-___5. The writer makes apt and specific reference to the text.

___-___6. The writer avoids plot summary not relevant to the explanation of the significant literary element.

___-___7. The writer discusses the literary work with sophistication, insight, and understanding.

___-___8. The writer displays consistent control over the language unique to the discussion of literature.

___-___9. The writer's diction, sentence structure, organization, and grammar aid in communicating a clear message.

MAXIMUM SCORE RESULTS: Grader 1 _____
MAXIMUM SCORE RESULTS: Grader 2 _____

STEP 2:   Check each item below which accurately describes the negative aspects of the essay being graded. This side describes how the essay may not be as good as the higher-scoring essays. (Grader one should check column one. Grader two should check column two):

___-___1. The writer's selection of a work of literary merit is not as appropriate as those of the higher-scoring essays.

___-___2. The writer's explanation of the meaning of the work is less thorough, less specific, or less perceptive than those of the higher-scoring essays.

___-___3. The writer's explanation of the significance of the literary element addressed in the question may be vague, underdeveloped, or misguided.

___-___4. The writer's explanation of how the literary element is significant to the work as a whole may be less convincing, mechanical, or inadequately related to the work as a whole.

___-___5. The writer's reference to the text lacks the specificity of the higher scoring essays.

___-___6. The writer simply paraphrases the meaning of the work with little reference to the significance of the literary element addressed in the question.

___-___7. The writer says nothing beyond the easy and obvious to grasp.

___-___8. The writer misuses the literary term(s) necessary to the discussion of literature or omits them partially or entirely.

___-___9. The essay contains distracting errors in grammar and mechanics.

RESULTS:

Grader 1: _____ - _____ = _____
                Step 1 Score   Step 2 Score

Grader 2: _____ - _____ = _____
                Step 1 Score   Step 2 Score

Grader 1 Score + Grader 2 Score = _____

Above sum /
divided by 2 =

Score for essay

AP Scoring for Tests

5 4 3 2 1

Student Name _____

The following represents a typical two-three week work load with typical AP conversions applied to arriving at a regular grade in the classroom.

Section I: Multiple-Choice:

_____ - (1/4 _____) X 1.35 =   _____   (67.5)

Number	Number	Weighted	Max
Right out of 50	Wrong	Section I	Possible
		Score	

Section II:
Free-Response:

_____ + _____ +_____ X 3.0556   = _____(82.5012)

Essay 1   Essay 2   2 wk   Weighted Score   Max
(9 point scale)   Theme   Section II)   Possible

Test Composite Score:

_____ + _____ =

Weighted Section I   Weighted Section II   **Composite Score**
Score   Score   (out of 150)

AP Grade:

AP Grade Conversion:

150 - 107	(71%)	5	A
106 - 93	(62%)	4	B
92 - 74	(49%)	3	C
73 - 44	(29%)	2	D
43 - 0		1	F

AP Scoring
for Homework

54321

Section III:

_____   _____ / _____
Name of Homework Activity   My points   Points Possible

Section IV:

_____   _____ / _____
Name of Homework Activity   My points   Points Possible

Section V:

_____   _____ / _____
Name of Homework Activity   My points   Points Possible

Homework Total Points =

Homework Composite/Ap Score/Grade
Fill in the Curve

_____-_____	(71%)	5	A
_____-_____	(62%)	4	B
_____-_____	(49%)	3	C
_____-_____	29%)	2	D
_____-_____		1	F

MY TOTALS:

_____ + _____ + _____ =
Previous   Test   Hmwk
Totals   Score   Score

My Grade=
Date=   (AP)   (Letter)
___-___-___

Write in curve below

_____-_____	(71%)	5	A
_____-_____	(62%)	4	B
_____-_____	(49%)	3	C
_____-_____	(29%)	2	D
_____-_____		1	F

*Use a pencil
for the
multiple-
choice
test!*

Chapter Three: Multiple Choice

Literature and Composition AP

Multiple Choice

Test-taking
Strategies &
Suggestions

The multiple-choice section of the exam consists of 50 to 60 questions on four passages which have to be answered in one hour. Full length practice tests are included in this booklet. Take these under real test conditions, allowing no more than one hour to complete the exam. Practice some of the strategies below and adopt those which work for you.

1. Become familiar with the directions. Those listed below are the same ones that are used on any AP multiple-choice exam.

> Directions: This part consists of selections from prose works and questions on their content, form, and style. After reading each passage, choose the best answer to each question and completely fill in the corresponding oval on the answer sheet. Note: Pay particular attention to the requirement of the questions that contain the words NOT, LEAST, or EXCEPT.

2. Skim over each passage before beginning. The questions do not need to be completed in any certain order. If the first passage seems difficult, skip it, looking for the easiest passage. After answering those easier questions, go on and complete as much of the exam as time allows. Note: If you do not start in the beginning, make sure to mark the answers in the right number on the oval answer sheets. Perhaps a good strategy here would be to mark the answers in the test booklet and then mark the corresponding ovals on the answer sheet after completing the entire exam.

3. Once you've selected a passage to begin, skim through the questions (but not the choices) so you know what to expect. Then, read the passage actively, circle items that seem to be addressed in the questions.

4. After reading the passage, read the questions, crossing out the obviously wrong answers. An answer will be wrong if it:

> A. Contradicts the passage

B. Is irrelevant to the passage
C. Is the same as one other choice and no test choice allows you to pick both as the right answer.

Note: Since any marked answer that is wrong costs an additional .25, leave the question blank unless you can make an "educated guess."

5. The questions are asked in the order that they appear in the passage, rather than by difficulty. A good strategy here would be to mark where each question is addressed in the passage. This will save time because you know that the next question will be after that in the passage.

6. Read all the choices before making a decision. Avoid selecting an answer, only to find out that an obviously better choice appeared that you did not even read.

7. Learn how to paraphrase the author's main ideas. Perhaps you will need to write the meaning down in the harder passages.

8. Manage your time by dividing each passage into 15 minute segments (four passages X 15 minutes = One hour). If you are having trouble with an answer, eliminate the obviously wrong answers by crossing them out on the answer booklet, skip the question and come back later within the same 15 minute period. It is too time consuming to have to rethink a question after reading another passage. Note: Be aware of the questions which include the words NOT, LEAST, or EXCEPT. In these cases, the right answer will be the one that does not apply to the passage.

9. See separate teacher's guide for answers and explanations for all multiple-choice tests in this book. Correct your test, analyzing your mistakes to avoid similar patterns in the future.

Multiple Choice
ABCDE

Collaborative
Writing
Directions

One of the best ways to learn how to score better on multiple-choice exams is to make multiple-choice exams. I have three AP sections, so I have each section write one class test. Step one begins in the first week and the final product is completed at the end of the marking period and used as the final test.

Step One: Individual Journal Entry Assignment

Each member of the class finds four well-written expository, descriptive, narrative, or persuasive passages from the AP suggested reading list in Chapter One. These excerpts should be written in the journal or word processed and submitted to the entire class for selection. One of the most effective ways to complete this assignment may be to surf the internet. Many of these authors have home pages that can be quickly printed. Just type in their name on any search engine on Net Scape and you'll be surprised at your results.

Step Two: Collaborative Assignment

The class reads the excerpts submitted by its members. The top four submissions are selected based on their literary worth and appropriateness. Students are then selected to word process and photocopy the submissions selected for use in their class's multiple choice test. The class is then divided into four passage groups, each group is assigned the task to write 20 questions on their passage.

Step Three: Individual Journal Entry Assignment

Each member of the class writes a separate, brief critical analysis of each of the three passages not assigned to their small group. These are submitted to the small group designated to work on that passage.

Step Four: Collaborative Assignment

Reading the critical analyses submitted on their passage, each small group member takes notes on the critical analyses read, discussing their content and assigning types of questions to each member. These written questions must emphasize the same variety as seen in the AP Typical Questions on pp. 64 - 75. Each small group member is assigned specific types of questions so the final small group submission of 20 questions will reflect the variety required.

Step Five: Individual Journal Writing Assignment

Each member of the small group is assigned an equal number of questions, but of the designated variety seen in the third number ratio in parentheses. One member might write three "vocabulary" questions and two "meaning" questions; another might write two "meaning" questions and three "dominant technique" questions, etc.

Step Six: Collaborative Assignment

The small group members share their results with their own group, selecting the top 12-15 for use in their class multiple choice test. These are then presented to the large group for acceptance. Note: Final selections of questions by the large group must reflect the variety indicated in the second number ratio in parentheses after each Typical Question on pp. 64 - 75. Students are then selected to word process the selected questions next to the already word processed and selected excerpts being used, arranging these questions in the order that they appear in the passage. When this is done, the test has to be photocopied so that each member of the class can do the next step.

Step Seven: Individual Assignment

Each member of the class is assigned an equal number of questions on passages not written by his/her group. An explanation for each question's answer has to be written.

Step Eight: Collaborative Assignment

The class discusses the answers and explanations to the questions read by the individual who wrote them, agreeing on any final changes.

Step Nine: Individual Assignment

Each member of the class takes notes on the discussion of the rationale for the right answer for the assigned questions, revising the explanation for the answers. Students then are assigned to put these explanations together in the order that they appear and photocopy them for distribution to the class that takes the test.

Step Ten: Collaborative Assignment

The class practices strategies listed on pp. 60 - 61 by taking the test written by another section, discussing the results when they are corrected, and making changes where poorly written questions or choices warrant a different best answer.

The following paraphrase of multiple-choice questions comes from the 1991 and 1994 *Advanced Placement Examination in English Literature and Composition and Its Grading* .

READING COMPREHENSION:

Vocabulary: Define words in context (1-2 out of 55)

1. In line 26, "what's disjunct" refers to something that ___

B. Narration / Point of View: Identify the speaker or the speaker's purpose OR attitude (4 out of 55)

1. The point of view in the passage is that of a
- (A) participating observer who is partial to someone
- (B) third person narrator who is aware of the main character's thoughts (central omniscient)
- (C) nonparticipating narrator who is unaware of the main character's thoughts (third person objective)
- (D) first person narrator who refers of himself in the third person
- (E) third person narrator who reveals the thoughts of several characters (Omniscient)

2. The narrator's attitude toward the main character can best be described as one of
- (A) Pity
- (B) Objectivity
- (C) Sardonic condemnation
- (D) Emotional Judgement
- (E) Jaded disgust.

3-4. The speaker of the passage is
- (A) a resentful victim
- (B) an unwelcome visitor
- (C) an ironic commentator
- (D) an curious investigator
- (E) an apologetic participant.

Pronoun/object reference: (2-3 out of 55)

1. In lines 28-29, the pronoun "it" in the phrase "it " refers to ___

D. Meaning: (12-15 out of 55)

1. It can be inferred from the phrase ". . ." that the speaker
- (A) dreaded ___
- (B) responded strongly but ambivalently to ___
- (C) found the ___ in the ___ mystifying and unpleasant
- (D) was indifferent to the emotional force that lay behind the ___
- (E) was disturbed by the insincerity of ___

2. The qualifiers "for them" and "so everyone said" suggests that the speaker

      (A) is confident that he will ___

      (B) shares the experience of those around him sym--pathetically

      (C) feels himself to be isolated from the rest of the people

      (D) views ___ as the ultimate authority over himself

      (E) is more interested in the experience of ___ than that of ___

4. Which of the following pairs of words refer to different entities?

      (A) "likeness" (line 1) and ""picture" (line 5)

      (B) "shadow" (line 8) and ""shadow" (line 12)

      (C) ""presence" (line 12) and ""presence" (line 10)

      (D) "picture" (line 16 and ""it" (line 8

      (E) "me" (line 23) and "picture" (line 24)

5. In the first stanza, the whippoorwill is presented chiefly as

      (A) a kind of poet

      (B) a symbol of death

      (C) an emblem of freedom

      (D) an annoyance

      (E) a messenger

6. The phrase "___" (line 6) emphasizes which of the following?

      (A) the delicacy of the ___

      (B) the brain's ability to conceive

      (C) the ___'s intuitive nature

      (D) the feminine nature of the artist

      (E) the need to be merciful

7. In the passage, ___ reflects on which of the following?

      (A) religion

      (B) other's misfortunes

      (C) escape

      (D) deposition

      (E) revenge

8. The speaker characterizes the life of the mountain village as

      (A) simple but rewarding

      (B) severe but patiently endured

      (C) enlightened by religion

      (D) wild as the surrounding landscape

      (E) cursed by both God and nature

Characterization: (6-7 out of 55)

1. Which of the following statements best defines ___'s relationship to ___?

    (A) ___ is only devoted to ___ out of a sense of moral obligation.

    (B) ___ makes a display of loving ___ because of a debt he owes ___.

    (C) ___ pretends to cherish ___ because he has designs on ___' inheritance.

    (D) ___ is unwilling to accept ___ because he holds a grudge against ___'s mother.

    (E) ___ treats ___ with disdain because he is jealous of ___.

2. Which of the following best describes the purpose of the last paragraph?

    (A) It illustrates how ___' political and family affairs reflect his character.

    (B) It counters speculations about ___'s character.

    (C) It shows how ___'s shortcomings are beneficial to his career.

    (D) It introduces ___'s role as an observer of ___'s actions.

    (E) It suggests the causes of ___'s moral transformation.

3. The narrator attributes ___'s attitude and behavior to which of the following factors?

    (A) lack of formal education

    (B) absence of religious beliefs

    (C) traits of his ancestors

    (D) social rank and flawed character

    (E) unsuccessful marriage and unprofitable projects

SOME OTHER CHARACTER TRAIT CHOICES INCLUDE: haughty condescension, uninhibited passions, misguided optimism, awkwardness, duplicity and capacity for treachery, social and political astuteness, verbal and rhetorical facility, single-minded intensity, narrow-minded prejudice, clear and unwavering judgment, inadequately compensated, used his position for selfish ends.

9. In the first paragraph, the speaker characterized the students primarily by describing their
    (A) attitudes
    (B) possessions
    (C) physical appearance
    (D) interactions with each other
    (E) interactions with their parents

10. The characters are described in terms of which of the following aspects of the lives?
    I. Social
    II. Physical
    III. Financial
    IV. Intellectual.

11. The characterization of ___ in lines 21-25 is marked by
    (A) hints of changes that will occur later
    (B) repetition of descriptive terms
    (C) implication about the nature of their lives
    (D) an emphasis on the alienation from the scene in the passage
    (E) a stress on the conflicts between ___ and ___

ORGANIZATION: (2-3 out of 55)

1. Which of the following best describes the order which objects are presented in paragraph one?
    (A) old to new
    (B) masculine to feminine
    (C) large to small
    (D) familiar to exotic
    (E) personal to impersonal

2. The words "invariably" (line 23 and "as always" (line 26) contribute which of the following to the development of the passage?
    I. They characterize the speaker as an experienced observer
    II. They introduce a sense of continuity relevant to the conclusion of the paragraph
    III. They provide an indirect comment on the description of the first paragraph

3. Which of the following best describes the organization of the passage?
    (A) specific descriptions leading to a generalization
    (B) illustration of an abstract idea by extended definition

      (C) application of a theory to a particular situation

      (D) amassment of imagery to convey a sense of chaos

      (E) narration of a series of events leading to a conflict

4. Which of the following indicates the major shift in the development of the speaker's exposition?

      (Use quoted lines as choices)

STYLE :

Literary Technique: (4-7 out of 55)

1. The STYLE of the passage as a whole can be best described as

      (A) humorless and pedantic

      (B) effusive and subjective

      (C) descriptive and metaphorical

      (D) terse and epigrammatic

      (E) witty and analytical

2. The image of "___" suggests all of the following EXCEPT

      (A) the energy generated by ___

      (B) the power of God in the Heavens

      (C) the swaying of ___ to the music

      (D) the cohesiveness and unity of the people

      (E) the despair of those who are bound to earth

3. The use of the word " ___ " is an example of which of the following? Some choices may include: exaggerated description, ironic reference, euphemism, allusion, metaphysical conceit, Biblical allusion, understatement, oxymoron, self-parody.

4. Which of the following lines contain an example of personification?

5. The dominant techniques in the first paragraph is the use of

      (A) hyperbole

      (B) puns

      (C) lists

      (D) euphemisms

      (E) abstraction

6. The first sentence of the passage is characterized by which of the following?

      (A) conventional metrical patterns

      (B) understatement and economy

      (C) romantic diction and imagery

      (D) periodic form and balance

      (E) sardonic mood and atmosphere

7. The first sentence of the passage is characterized by all of the following EXCEPT:

    (A) multiple modifiers

    (B) parallel structures

    (C) oppressive atmosphere

    (D) religious imagery

    (E) ironic wit

8. In the passage, the ___ functions as

    (A) a symbol of the ___'s plight

    (B) an image of the charm of the ___

    (C) a comparison of work with leisure

    (D) an emblem of the ___'s influence

    (E) a metaphor for the ___'s leisure

9. Which of the following are the most prominent IMAGES in the poem?

    (A) darkness, light, and the cross

    (B) fellowship, prayer, and rebirth

    (C) silence, nature, and music

    (D) sowing, reaping, and animal husbandry

    (E) movement and growth

B. Diction: (3 out of 55)

1. The diction used to describe ___ in lines 9-21 suggests that

    (A) Science is slowly beginning to understand certain mysteries.

    (B) The speaker finds some aspects of nature alien to her.

    (C) Nature is able to provide a truly magical spectacle.

    (D) Nature is governed by a higher power.

    (E) The beauty of nature is a source of comfort to the speaker.

2. The two quotations in lines 15-17 are seen by the speaker as

    (A) contradictory

    (B) comforting

    (C) absurd

    (D) trite

    (E) clever

C. Syntax (Sentence Structure) (0-1 out of 55)

1. The style of the passage as a whole can be characterized by

    (A) simple declarative sentences containing a minimum of descriptive language

    (B) complex sentences interspersed with short, exclamatory statements

      (C) sentences that contain several modifying phrases and subordinate clauses

      (D) sentences that grow progressively more argumentative as the passage progresses

      (E) Expository sentences at the beginning that give way to interpretive sentences at the end

Effect: (2-3 out of 55)

1. In lines 12-14, the words "____" have which of the following effects?

      (A) They retard the tempo of the speaker's prose.

      (B) They satirize ____.

      (C) They highlight the distractions that spoil the audience's concentration.

      (D) They change, for a moment, the point of view of the speaker.

      (E)

2. Which of the following best describes the effect produced by the phrase "____"?

      (A) It signals to the reader that ____ is an unpleasant event.

      (B) It emphasizes how vague ____'s memory is.

      (C) It establishes the contrast between ____'s past and future.

      (D) It emphasizes the pervasiveness of ____ in ____'s memory.

      (E) It alerts the reader to ____'s naivete.

3. Which of the following best describes the effect produced by the repetition of the words "seeming" and "seemed" throughout the passage?

      (A) It serves to emphasize ____'s particular perspective on (a certain subject).

      (B) It functions as a reminder to the reader that the narrator is only telling a story.

      (C) It suggests that ____'s memory of the events are vague and indistinct.

      (D) It provides support for the extended allegory developed in the passage.

      (E) It highlights the speaker's capacities as an omniscient narrator.

4. The chief effect of the diction in the sentence "____" (lines 25-27) is to provide

      (A) a vivid contrast to the description of ____

(B) a strong emphasis on the life of grinding hardship introduced in the sentence "___" (lines 23-24)

(C) an ironic commentary on the villagers who do not possess the virtues of "Love, patience, faith, hospitality"

(D) an elevated romantic atmosphere that enhances the attitude of the speaker

(E) a sense of despair and defeat that is inflicted on the villagers by a vengeful deity

Tone: (4-6 out of 55)

1. The IRONY in the passage as a whole rest chiefly in the conflict between

(A) the solemnity of the occasion and the joy of the worshippers

(B) ___'s prophetic wrath and his mother's long suffering

(C) the air of expectancy and the sounds from the street

(D) ___'s acute observation of (a happening) and his inability to participate in it

(E) the change that takes place in the characters and their outward appearance.

4. Which of the following is an irony presented in the poem?

(A) The ___, apparently under control, is a threat to ___ .

(B) The ___, once in awe of ___, has learned to impose her will on it.

(C) The speaker, able to understand the position of ___, can not comprehend that of ___.

(D) The ___, once a powerful hunter, has now become a prey.

(E) The ___, through her mastery of ___, has gained the ability to control her own thoughts.

TWO WORD EXAMPLES OF TONE:

playful seriousness, ironic grimness, cheerful glee, somber melancholy, irreversible despair

ADJECTIVE EXAMPLES OF TONE:

inspiring, comforting, unfathomable, vicious, benign

NOUN EXAMPLES OF TONE:

regret, awe, tragedy, hope, danger, meanspiritedness, vengeance, amusement, cynicism, disinterestedness, detachment, condescension, pity, enthusiasm, hope

Rhetorical Purpose: (5-6 out of 55)

1. The depiction of ___'s " ___" and his mother's " ___" serves what specific function in the narrative progress of the passage?
  - (A) It diverts the reader's attention from ___'s point of view.
  - (B) It retards the pace of the narration prior to the climax.
  - (C) It provides a specific example of a preceding general description.
  - (D) It counters earlier references to ___.
  - (E) It offers a parallel to the transformation that the main character undergoes in the passage.

2. The attention the speaker pays to the details of sound serve primarily to
  - (A) distract the reader from the disconcerting issues raised in the passage
  - (B) offer the reader a physical sense of ___
  - (C) construct a metaphor for ___'s relationship to ___
  - (D) entertain the reader prior to the presentation of more challenging material
  - (E) complement the attention paid to the visual and the tactile

3. A principal purpose of the word "shadow" (line 12) is to
  - (A) foreshadow the departure of the speaker
  - (B) emphasize the disintegration of the picture
  - (C) serve as a balance for the use of " ___"
  - (D) compensate for the negative connotation of " ___"
  - (E) contrast with the meaning of " ___"

4. In context, the phrases " ___" (line 29), " ___" (line 25),   and " ___" (lines 44-45) serve to
  - (A) evoke an otherworldly atmosphere resonant of the Bible
  - (B) situate the passage within a socially conservative framework
  - (C) highlight the bitter, sardonic humor of the passage
  - (D) mask the passage's truly secular emphasis
  - (E) endorse a particular approach to spiritual matters

5. Lines 44-43 have all of the following functions EXCEPT to
  - (A) return to the initial subject of the poem
  - (B) illustrate the influence of childhood experience
  - (C) link the present to the past

    (D) emphasizes the chaotic quality of natural events

    (E) evoke a family relationship

6. The primary rhetorical purpose of the passage is to

    (A) characterize a group of people

    (B) defend the value of a certain lifestyle

    (C) dramatize the importance of various possessions

    (D) illustrate the variety of amusements valued by
         most people

    (E) condemn ___'s attitudes toward ___

7. It can be inferred that the rhythm and diction of the concluding lines are intended to reflect

    (A) ___'s philosophy of life

    (B) the speaker's deep-seated beliefs

    (C) an objective summary of the day's events

    (D) ___'s views of his/her own importance

    (E) the outsider's scorn for ___.

8. The function of the sentences beginning "___" (line 23) is to

    (A) provide examples of ___

    (B) defend the ___' lack of ___

    (C) contradict the preceding observations about beauty
         and knowledge

    (D) illustrate the ___'s appreciation for ___

    (E) enumerate the simple joys of ___

9. The description "___" serves to

    (A) recall the necessity of learning and action

    (B) qualify a previous generalization about ___

    (C) emphasize the complete hopelessness of ___

    (D) illustrate the self-confidence and optimism of ___

    (E) contradict earlier statements about ___ in the passage.

10. The central rhetorical strategy of the passage is to

    (A) allow the reader to form individual judgments

    (B) undercut the speaker's statements with irony

    (C) imitate the language of a certain group of people

    (D) begin and end on a note of uncertainty

    (E) contrast the setting and its inhabitants

Chapter Four:

Poetry

Literature and Composition AP

Poetry-Literature and Composition

Poetry Questions

Students are encouraged by all AP English Instructors to write often. The types of questions that follow are designed to give students practice in brainstorming and to encourage exploration and experimentation. As such, these are not graded with the same type of specific content and mechanics checklists used for AP-type essay exams. In fact, I grade these assignments on two criteria: quantity and variety. I award two points per page (up to 15 pages), but they must select from three of the following categories:

1. Chapter Three: Collaborative Writing
2. Chapter Four, Five or Six: Poetry Questions/Prose Questions/or Drama Questions (Whichever is appropriate to the genre they are reading)
3. Chapter Seven: Creative Suggestions
4. Chapter Eight: Writing Prompts

How to Read and Interpret Poetry

The AP Literature essay question on poetry will always ask the writer to make a connection between two things: how the poet uses **language** to create **tone** or **meaning**.

First, read the question carefully to determine what you have to define. It will either be what is the speaker's attitude, view of self, assumptions, or intentional effects; or what is the poem's meaning. Since AP poems are selected because of their complexity, it is good to begin by discussing the deliberate ambiguities in attitude or meaning which allow for multiple interpretations in the first paragraph of your essay. Also, these different interpretations may form the basis for your organization.

Secondly, analyze how the language is used to create that tone or meaning. Some of these language devices could include such things as imagery, phrasing, sentence structure, verse form, organization of the poem, or selection of details.

The body of the essay may be organized on the different language devices used by the author or the multiple interpretations of the author's attitude. Never force a set organizational model into an assigned poem. Rather, organize the analysis based on the poem and the directives given to you by the question. Use the following three-step approach to determine the best way to write the essay. Determine the meaning or tone of the poem, determine how the meaning or tone is created by the poet's manipulation of the language, and relate this to the effect it has on the reader.

Three Close Reading Steps for Analyzing Poetry:

I. DETERMINE THE LITERAL MEANING (DOMINANT IMPRESSION OR TONE) OF THE POEM:
  A. Situational Context:
      1. Who is the speaker(s)?
      2. What kind of person is the speaker?
      3. What is the topic spoken about in the situation / setting ?
      4. What is the occasion: Event, Time (hour, season, century)
      5. What is the location (one or several?- indoors or out, urban or rural, land or sea, region, country, or hemisphere) ?
      6. What is the conflict, if any ? Comparison and contrast? Dilemma?
      7. What are the key images / types of sensory experiences (sight, sound, etc.) Groupings of images?
      8. What is the central theme or idea of the poem and how is it achieved?
  B. Type of poem:
      1. Descriptive (imagery without a story).
      2. Narrative (the ballad, dramatic monologue, epic).
      3. Lyrical (expressive of emotional states;

songlike).

4. Topical (poetic essays, commentaries, etc.).

C. Purpose - Which of the following purposes does the poem seem to have?

1. To stress ideas offering insight into human nature and situations or into abstract ideas.

2. To tell a story.

3. To express an emotion.

4. To create a mood or atmosphere.

5. To describe a person, scene or thing

6. To amuse.

7. To satirize.

D. Imagery:

1. Is the poem free of images? Does direct language dominate the poem?

2. Does the poet primarily use purely descriptive images, those that appeal to the senses?

3. Is the imagery based on association (the psychological process whereby you are led to link two elements)?

4. Do the images fall into patterns related to the meaning? Do these patterns in effect become dominant symbols lifting the reader beyond the literal level?

II. DETERMINE HOW THE POEM ACHIEVES THIS DOMINANT IMPRESSION. WHAT TYPE OF LANGUAGE DOES THE POET USE TO CREATE THE VISION AND THE VOICE DETERMINED IN STEP I?

A. Poetic Devices:

1. Does one symbol, allegorical device, simile, metaphor or personification seem to dominate the poem?

2. Research any allusions made.

3. What imagery is seen by the combination of all the figurative language used?

4. How does the poet's tone (attitude) bring emotional power to the poem?

5. What sounds contribute to the overall effect of the poem?

B. Language, phrasing and diction:

1. What general term would you use to describe the author's choice of words - artificial and stilted, highly ornate, Latinate, archaic, abstract, conversational, colloquial, rhetorical, sentimental, intensely emotional, trite, etc?

2. Which words are particularly well-chosen, why?

3. What repetitions, synonyms, adjectives, etc. are directly related to attitudes and the poet's tone?

4. Does the author rely heavily on unusual words? Why?

5. Does he rely heavily on simple colloquial language? Why?

6. What words seem significant - connotative or suggestive of figurative meaning? How are these words related to the context?

7. Does the poet's desire to present musical effects (meter or rhyme) influence his choice of words? If the influence is heavy, is the quality of the poem marred?

8. Does the poet's place in time or environment have anything to do with the words he uses? Do any of the words have different meanings today?

9. Can you substitute words of your own for some used by the poet? Which are better? Why? Does this experiment help you understand the difference between poetic diction and ordinary diction?

10. What language is literal ? Figurative?

    a. Can you paraphrase the poem on a literal level?

    b. Is there any evidence (such as key words, repetition of symbols, images, etc.) which leads you to suspect that the poem must be taken beyond paraphrase?

    c. Does the poet's tendency to compress material create the possibility of multiple interpretations?

d. Are there deliberate ambiguities which allow for multiple interpretations?

11. Is there any ironic language (opposite of the usual literal meaning), sarcasm, dramatic irony;, paradox, Serious vs. Comic language?

12. Other aspects of language

a. Unfamiliar words (look up in dictionary).

b. Allusions (look up in an encyclopedia).

c. Foreign words, phrases (look up in an Oxford Dictionary).

d. Sound patterns (see also meter below), meaning conveyed or reinforced by sound (alliteration or assonance or consonance).

C. Verse form is described by its meter (syllable pattern) and feet (number of repetitions of the same syllable pattern). For instance, *iambic pentameter* has five iambs in a line.

1. Types of verse: iambic, dactylic, trochaic, anapestic

a. Iambic meter- A metrical foot consisting of one unstressed syllable followed by one stressed syllable.

b. Dactylic meter - A metrical foot consisting of one accented syllable followed by two unaccented syllables.

c. Trochaic meter- A metrical foot consisting of one stressed syllable followed by one unstressed syllable.

d. Anapestic meter- A metrical foot consisting of two unaccented syllables followed by one accented syllable.

2. Types of feet:

a. monometer- a metrical line containing one foot.

        b. dimeter- a metrical line containing two feet.

        c. trimeter- a metrical line containing three feet.

        d. tetrameter- a metrical line containing four feet.

        e. pentameter- a metrical line containing five feet.

        f. hexameter- a metrical line containing six feet.

        g. heptameter- a metrical line containing seven feet.

        h. octometer- a metrical line containing eight feet.

3. Rhyme scheme (pattern).
4. Refrain (line repetitions).
5. Stanza forms:

        a. Couplet- two rhyming lines.

        b. Triplet (tercet)- three rhyming lines.

        c. Terza rima- three lines, but only the first and last lines rhyme.

        d. Quatrain- four lines with any combination of rhyme schemes.

D. Free Verse (Is the pattern irregular enough to be called free verse?):

    1. Poetry that has no regular rhyme or rhythm is free verse.

    2. Free verse relies instead on the natural rhythms of ordinary speech.

    3. Poets writing in free verse may use alliteration, internal rhyme, onomatopoeia, or other musical devices to achieve their effects.

    4. Most poets of free verse place great emphasis on imagery.

E. Musical Characteristics - *Rhythm:*

    1. Can you determine a pattern of stress? Does this pattern fit any of the traditional patterns such as iambic?

    2. Does the pattern vary? If so, are these variations due to carelessness or do they have pur-

pose (in terms of meaning, emotional intensity, etc.)?

3. What functions do pauses perform in the sound pattern?

4. Are there run-on lines? What effect do these have? How are syntax, syllabication, punctuation, or the lack of punctuation related to sound?

5. Does the purpose and/or meaning of the poem or of a given item or passage help you determine how it should be read (tone of voice, pitch, speed of delivery, etc.).

6. If the music is entirely regular or even monotonous, is this quality due to the failure of the poet or to a purpose which is supported by the poem?

F. Musical Characteristics - *Rhyme:*

1. Is there a rhyme scheme? Is it dictated by convention or is it original?

2. What relevance does the rhyme have to the music of the poem? Does it help or impede the sound pattern?

3. Are there irregular rhymes? If so, why? Are they due to chronological changes in the pronunciation of the words or the poet's desire to pun?

4. If there is no rhyme, is the author using a traditional pattern like blank verse, or does he have some other reason to avoid rhyme. Blank verse is written in unrhymed iambic pentameter (each line contain five iambs or feet, consisting of an unstressed syllable followed by a stressed syllable). William Shakespeare uses blank verse.

5. Is internal rhyme used? Why?

6. Does rhyme or absence of rhyme contribute anything to your understanding of the poem?

G. Other Musical Characteristics:

1. Does the poet use any of the following musical devices: alliteration (repetition of initial consonant sounds); assonance (repetition of

similar vowel sounds followed by different consonant sounds); consonance (repetition of final consonant sounds after different vowel sounds); onomatopoeia (the use of a word whose sound imitates or suggests its meaning); parallelism (the repetition of words, phrases, or sentences that have the same grammatical structure)?

H. Verse Form

1. Ballad- The typical ballad stanza is a quatrain with the rhyme scheme *abcb*. The second and third line have three stressed syllables; the first and third lines have four stressed syllables. Often the meter is primarily iambic.

2. Epic- A long narrative poem, written in grand language, about a larger than life hero who embodies the values of a society. Included are elements of myth, folklore, history, and legend. Homer's *Odyssey* and *Iliad* and Virgil's *Aeneid,* as well as the Anglo-Saxon poem *Beowulf* and Milton's *Paradise Lost* are among the best known epics.

3. Lyric Poetry- poem which focuses on emotions and thoughts rather than on telling a story. John Keats's "To Autumn" and Matthew Arnold's "Dover Beach" are two of the most famous lyrical poems.

4. Ottava Rima- A poem with an eight-line stanza in iambic pentameter with the rhyme scheme *abababcc*. Lord Byron's *Don Juan* and William Butler Yeat's "Sailing to Byzantium" are two famous examples of this verse form.

5. Pastoral- A type of poem that depicts rural life in idealized terms, or that expresses a nostalgia for a past age of innocence.

6. Sonnet - A 14 line lyric poem. There are three major types:

a. Petrarchan (Italian)- This sonnet is divided into two parts: an eight line octave with the rhyme scheme *abbaabba* and a six line sestet with the rhyme scheme *cdcdcd* or *cdecde*. In most Italian sonnets the octave describes a situation and the sestet describes a change in the situation. The change is called the turn. The turn signals a logical shift or new beginning. Sometimes the first part presents a problem, poses a question, or expresses an idea, which the sestet then resolves, answers or drives home. Sometimes the problem is intensified in the sestet with a new solution given. John Keats's "On First Looking Into Chapman's Homer" is an example of an Italian sonnet (See Practice Test Two- Essay one).

b. Shakespearean or English sonnet- This form has three four line units (quatrains), ending with a two line unit (couplet). The organization of thought usually corresponds to this form. The three quatrains usually express similar ideas or examples, and the couplet expresses the concluding message. The most common rhyme scheme is *abab cdcd efef gg*.

c. Spenserian Sonnet- This sonnet, like the Shakespearean sonnet, is divided into three quatrains and a couplet, but its rhyme scheme links the quatrains: *abab bcbc cdcd ee*

7. Spenserian Stanza- a nine line stanza with a rhyme scheme *ababbcbcc*. The first eight lines are in iambic pentameter, and the ninth line is in Alexandrine (a line of iambic hexameter). Several Romantic poets have used this stanza form.

8. Villanelle- a nineteen line poem divided into five tercets (three-line stanzas), each with the rhyme scheme *aba*, and a final quatrain with the rhyme scheme *abaa*. Line one is repeated entirely to form lines six, 12, and 18.

Line three is repeated as lines nine, 15, and 19. The two lines used as refrains (line one and three) are paired as the final couplet. Dylan Thomas's "Do Not Go Gentle Into the Good Night" is an example of a modern villanelle.

III. SO WHAT?

This is the part that makes the highest scores. Somehow you must attach an individual response to your analysis. This should be done throughout the written analysis, and certainly makes a good strategy for an effective ending.

A. How do the above devices affect the reader?

B. What sort of difference does this poem make in the lives of the readers?

C. Does it communicate some new experience or some fresh understanding of the familiar?

D. Does it express something we have experienced but have no words to describe?

E. Does the poem engage a combination of the senses, imagination, intellect, and emotion?

Chapter Five:

Prose

Literature and Composition AP

Prose-Literature and Composition
Novel/Short Story Questions

Students are encouraged by all English AP Instructors to write often. The types of questions that follow are designed to give students practice in brainstorming and to encourage exploration and experimentation. As such, these are not graded with the same type of specific content and mechanics check-lists used for AP-type essay exams. In fact, I grade these assignments on two criteria: quantity and variety. I award two points per page (up to 15 pages), but they must select from three of the following categories:

1. Chapter Three: Collaborative Writing
2. Chapter Four, Five or Six: Poetry Questions/Prose Questions/or Drama Questions (Whichever is appropriate to the genre they are reading)
3. Chapter Seven: Creative Suggestions
4. Chapter Eight: Writing Prompts

How to Read and Interpret Prose

The AP Literature essay question on prose, like poetry, will always ask the writer to make a connection between two things: how the author uses **language** to create **tone** or **meaning**.

First, read the question carefully to determine what you have to define. It will either be what is the author's (or character's) attitude, view of self, assumptions, or intentional effects; or what is the passage's meaning. Since AP prose passages are selected because of their complexity, it is good to begin by discussing the deliberate ambiguities in attitude or meaning which allow for multiple interpretations in the first paragraph of your essay. Also, these different interpretations may form the basis for your organization.

Secondly, analyze how the language is used to create

that tone or meaning. Some of these language devices could include such things as imagery, phrasing, sentence structure, organization, or selection of details.

The body of the essay may be organized on the different language devices used by the author or the multiple interpretations of the author's attitude. Never force a set organizational model into an assigned poem. Rather, organize the analysis based on the passage and the directives given to you by the question. Use the following three-step approach to determine the best way to write the essay. Determine the meaning or tone of the passage, determine how the meaning or tone is created by the author's manipulation of the language, and relate this to the effect it has on the reader.

Three Close Reading Steps
for Analyzing Prose Passages:

I. DETERMINE THE LITERAL TONE, ATTITUDE, POINT OF VIEW OR MEANING OF THE PASSAGE:
   A. Conflict
      1. Does the story have important external conflicts? Do the characters struggle against some outside force (another character, society as a whole, or some natural force)?
      2. Does the story have important internal conflicts? Do the characters struggle within self between opposing needs, opposing desires, or opposing emotions?
   B. Setting (The time, place, environment, and surrounding circumstances)
      1. Does the setting contribute to the story's emotional effect?
      2. Does the setting reveal the story's conflict?
      3. Does the setting reveal characterization?
   C. Tone, Point of view, or attitude
      1. What is the author's tone?
      2. Who is telling the story? What is the point of view?
      3. What is the main character's attitude?

D. Theme

1. A theme is not the same as the subject of a work, which can usually be stated in a word or two. Theme is the central idea or insight of the work . . . the idea the author wishes to convey about the subject . . . the writer's view of the world or revelation about human nature. While some themes are directly stated most are implied. It is up to the reader to piece together all the clues the writer has provided about the work's total meaning. Almost all good novels and short stories have some editorializing . . . times in which the author steps outside the story line and directly states the theme. Two of the most important clues to consider, when the theme is implied, are:

    a. how the main character has changed

    b. how the conflict has been resolved.

2. Does the story communicate some meaningful insight into human nature or life?

3. Does the theme deal with important aspects of life? Does it present a new idea or an accepted truth?

4. What subject dealt with helps to understand the generalization the author wants us to make about life? (old age, ambition, love, prejudice, good vs. evil, distorted views of women, mob justice, religion, money, guilt, courage, etc.)

II. DETERMINE HOW THE AUTHOR USES THE LANGUAGE TO CREATE THE TONE, POINT OF VIEW, OR MEANING:

A. Plot

1. Does the story have unity? Do all the basic elements (conflict, characterization, setting, theme, point of view, and stylistic devices) create a logical purpose or effect?

B. Characterization

Do the characters:

1. Exhibit a good reason for being there?

2. Talk as human beings would talk in a given circumstance?

3. Have a discoverable purpose?

4. Have a show of relevancy?

Are the people:

1. Interesting ?

2. Properly described? Does their conduct and conversation fit these descriptions?

3. Confine themselves to possibilities and let miracles alone?

4. Elicit empathy from the reader?

Are the characters in the story

1. Part typical,

2. Part universal,

3. Part individual, and

4. Consistent throughout the story.

C. Narration

1. What are the advantages or disadvantages of the author's choice of narration?

2. Is the point of view consistent? If not, does the writer have a good reason for switching the point of view?

D. Some Literary and Stylistic Elements to consider

1. Does the writer keep the reader's interest by having some:

a. Foreshadowing

b. Humor

c. Excitement

d. Element of originality

e. Development of mystery and tragedy

2. Does the writer "say what he wants to say, not merely come near it" (Twain) by:

a. Using the right word, not its second cousin.

b. "Eschewing surplusage."

c. Including all necessary details.

d. Avoiding slovenliness.

3. How does the author's use of the following stylistic and rhetorical devices contribute to the story's overall tone, point of view, attitude or meaning?

1. Syntax (Sentence Structure)
2. Satire
3. Poetical devices (Figures of Speech)
4. Symbols
5. Imagery

E. Romanticism: Is the writing Romantic because it displays some of the following characteristics?

1. *Romantic literature* is more imaginative than real: Some people or things are not believable.

2. *Romantic literature* usually pictures an ideal world.

3. *Romantic literature* shows a lot of emotions.

4. *Romantic literature* uses a lot of exaggeration or fabrication that has no real substance.

5. *Romantic literature* has a sympathetic interest in "primitive nature."

6. *Romantic literature* has a sympathetic interest in "Medievalism" (the beliefs of the people in European History between 476 A.D.-1450 A.D.

7. *Romantic literature* is barbarous, uncivilized.

8. *Romantic literature* uses a medieval setting, atmosphere, etc. to suggest horror and mystery.

9. *Romantic literature* uses artificially lofty diction and syntax.

10. *Romantic literature* has a great interest in the picturesque aspects of the past.

F. Naturalism: Does the writing have some of the following characteristics of Naturalism?

1. Characters are doomed to lose because of heredity and environment.

2. The two opposing forces are unequal. Heredity and environment are too much against the protagonist so it is a losing battle.

3. Typical topics for stories include:
    a. Poverty
    b. War
    c. The life and death struggle

d. The deceit and irresponsibility between men and women
e. The law of the jungle
f. Child abuse
g. Unrequited love

4. The characters have some sort of intense
pressure which causes some sort of detachment.

5. Naturalistic stories are unrelenting explo-
sions of evil grossly exaggerated.

G. Realism: Is the writing Realistic because it displays some of the following characteristics?

1. The author goes to great lengths to make
the setting historically accurate.

2. The setting is contemporary to the time it
was written.

3. The characters are fully portrayed as part
typical, part universal, part individual, and
therefore plausible (believable).

4. The two opposing forces are equal in the
conflict, making for a suspenseful plot.

5. The conflict is solved in a believable manner.

6. The characters speak as real people speak.

III. SO WHAT?

This is the part that makes the highest scores. Somehow you
must attach an individual response to your analysis. This
should be done throughout the written analysis, and it certainly makes a good strategy for an effective ending.

A. Plot

1. Is the plot believable and natural, or does
it seem contrived? Does it rely too much on
coincidence and chance?

2. Is the ending satisfying or does it seem a
cliche ending?

3. Is the story suspenseful? Is the writer's
purpose simply to entertain with a "thriller,"
or does the plot involve complex issues and

behavior?

4. Does the tale accomplish something and arrive somewhere?

5. Are all episodes a necessary development of the tale?

B. Conflict

1. Is the conflict significant? If it's significant, it can't be easily resolved. If it's significant, the crisis changes the lives of the characters involved.

2. Are the two opposing forces equal in strength? If the outcome is never in question, the reader loses interest.

C. Setting

1. Is the setting believable?

D. Characterization

1. Are the characters believable?

2. Are their motivations (the reasons for their actions) clear and believable? Do they behave consistently?

3. Do any of the characters change or develop during the course of the story?

4. To what extent does your story concentrate on the hidden characteristics of the characters?

5. To what extent is this a story of ordinary men and women living ordinary lives, frittering away their time on petty activities?

6. To what extent is this a story of individuals of intensity who awaken our sense of the potential of humans?

E. Theme

1. Does the theme seem believable?

2. Does it relate to human life as I know it?

Chapter Six:

Drama

Literature and Composition AP

Drama-Literature and Composition

Students are encouraged by all English AP Instructors to write often. The types of questions that follow are designed to give students practice in brainstorming and encourage exploration and experimentation. As such, these are not graded with the same type of specific content and mechanics checklists used for AP-type essay exams. In fact, I grade these assignments on two criteria: quantity and variety. I award two points per page (up to 15 pages), but they must select from three of the following categories:

1. Chapter Three: Collaborative Writing
2. Chapter Four, Five or Six: Poetry Questions/Prose Questions/or Drama Questions (Whichever is appropriate to the genre they are reading)
3. Chapter Seven: Creative Suggestions
4. Chapter Eight: Writing Prompts

How to Read and Interpret Drama

The AP Literature essay exam addresses drama only in the open or "free choice" question. Here you are asked to show how one specifically listed part of a suitable play or novel functions in the novel or play as a whole. To do this you must:

A. Provide a reasonable explanation of the meaning of the work selected, and

B. Make apt and specific references to the text which explains how that specifically listed part contributes to the meaning of the work as a whole. To get a high score here, as with the other essays, you must also

C. Attach an individual response that explains the "So What" aspect of the question.

The following questions are designed to help you in this task:

I. PROVIDE A REASONABLE EXPLANATION OF THE MEANING OF THE WORK:

  A. Plot: Will a brief summary of the plot make the meaning clear?

  B. Types of Drama:

    1. Is your play a comedy?

      a. Is the audience amused?

      b. Does the action show a movement from unhappiness to happiness, entertaining rather than distressing the audience?

      c. Does the play appeal to the intellect?

    2. Is your play a tragedy?

      a. Does a great person come to an unhappy or disastrous end, often through some lapse in judgment or character flaw?

      b. Does the play appeal to the emotions?

  C. Characterization: In drama, the characters tell the tale through their dialogue and actions. There must not be too many people on stage at any one time, for if the stage is too crowded, the audience may not be able to follow the action. In Greek Drama, for instance, each playwright was limited to three speaking actors. There is no limit to the number of nonspeaking, walk-on parts. Consider the following important aspects of characterization:

    1. Antagonist- who is the person (the bad guy) or a force (such as the weather) that opposes the protagonist?

    2. Archetype- Is there an image, story pattern or character type which occurs frequently enough in literature to be recognizable?

    3. Does the Protagonist (the good guy) receive the sympathies of the reader because the events center around him/her, or because the narrator is sympathetic toward him/her?

    4. Does a character act as a foil (a character who, through contrast, shows the character-

istics of a major character)?

D. Empathy-

    1. Does the audience identify with the characters to establish the dramatists desired relationships?

    2. Does the audience feel sympathy for the major characters (we must be emotionally affected by the fate of these characters if the play is to be successful)?

    3. Is the audience made to feel that the characters have good reasons for doing what they do?

E. Dialogue- In a play, what is said and how it is said are next in importance to character

    1. Is the dialogue accurate?

    2. Through dialogue can we learn what is going through a character's mind? (A Dramatic Monologue is a long speech used to reveal a character's thoughts.)

    3. Is the dialogue believable?

F. Theme- What is the main idea that the writer of the literary work wants to convey to the reader? What is the writer's view of the world or revelation about human nature?

    1. Antithesis- Does the playwright make a contrast of ideas expressed in a grammatically balanced statement?

    2. Irony- Is there any contrast or discrepancy between what is expected and what actually is?

        a. Verbal Irony- Does a character say one thing and mean the opposite?

        b. Situational Irony- Is what actually happens the opposite of the expected?

        c. Dramatic Irony- Does the audience know something important that a character in the story or play does not know?

G. Motif- Does a word, character, object, image, metaphor, or idea recur?

H. Effect: Edgar Allan Poe's "Single Effect" Theory: Even though Poe's single effect theory refers to a short

story, drama also needs to produce a "single effect."
In his famous review of Nathaniel Hawthorne's *Twice Told Tales* (1842), Poe laid down the rules for what has come to be called the "well-made tale."

1. Does the writer try to establish a preconceived "single effect"? Does he create events that will best aid him in establishing that effect? Does every word add to that effect? (The effect desired by watching a tragedy is one of catharsis.)

2. The length of a short story should be "one sitting" - one to two hours. Does this time limit, imposed on all plays, pose any problems for your play?

3. The effect Poe sought to create was terror, passion, or horror. Does your tragedy have the same effects?

II. MAKE APT AND SPECIFIC REFERENCES TO THE TEXT WHICH EXPLAIN HOW THAT SPECIFICALLY LISTED PART CONTRIBUTES TO THE MEANING OF THE WORK AS A WHOLE:

A. Structure: Plot: explain the progression of action by writing a summary of each of the following:

1. **Exposition**: Where and how does the playwright introduce the characters, setting, and the story's major conflict? Is there some interesting element, a narrative hook, that draws the reader into the story?

2. **Complication**: What developments intensify the conflict? Does each event in the plot relate to conflict? Is there any evidence of foreshadowing? All good writing has cleverly written "hints about future events" which help the reader maintain an active interest in the story.

3. **Turning Point**: In drama, one type of climatic moment is the turning point or crisis. In Shakespeare's plays, this moment usually occurs in the third act. The turning point is the pivotal moment when the hero's fortunes begin to decline or improve.

4. **Climax**: What is the high point of the story? What happens to resolve the conflict, ending the story? In Shakespeare's plays, the climax usually occurs in the last act, just before the final scene.

5. **Falling action**: How are the mysteries or problems of the plot unraveled?

6. **Catastrophe** (the ending of a tragedy): OR

6. **Denouement** (ending of a comedy):

B. Scene: Does the division of an act indicate a
    1. Stage of action?
    2. Shift in place?
    3. Change in the number of players on stage?

C. Stage Direction: the dramatists written directions
    1. How the scenes are to be set?
    2. How are lines to be spoken?

D. Character Development-
    1. Does the protagonist learn from the tragedy inflicted upon him and become a more likable person?
    2. Does the plot involve inner or outer conflict and some kind of decision?
    3. Does the main character choose to perform or not to perform some morally meaningful act that will lead to the play's resolution?
    4. Does the action involve a noble person who, because of a "tragic flaw," makes a wrong decision which leads to an unhappy catastrophe?
    5. Does the experience, although disastrous, deepen the hero's insight into his/her own nature and destiny?

III. SO WHAT? To get a high score here, as with the other essays, you must also attach an individual response that explains the "So What" aspect of the question.

A. In his *Philosophy of Composition*, published in 1846, Poe established that the aim of the story was to include, not only truth (the satisfaction of the intellect) but also passion (the excitement of the heart). Are these aims accomplished in your play?

B. Does the tragedy have some catharsis? In feeling pity and fear for the tragic hero, are the viewer's own tensions released and temporarily resolved?

C. What sort of difference does this play make in the lives of the audience?

D. Does it communicate some new experience or some fresh understanding of the familiar?

E. Does it express something we have experienced but have no words to describe?

E. Does the play engage a combination of the senses, imagination, intellect, and emotion?

A Doll's House by **Henrik Ibsen**

An Act is one of the major divisions of a play; it usually marks a stage in the development of the action. In ancient Greek and Roman plays, the action could generally be divided into five stages of dramatic development: exposition, complication, climax, falling action, and catastrophe (the ending of a tragedy) or denouement (ending of a comedy). The actual division of a play into five stages, which came later, was an attempt to formally indicate this basic structure.

Modern playwrights, however, have come to divide their plays according to their own unique structure rather than attempting to follow this rather abstract pattern.

1. Why did Ibsen divide his plays into three acts?
2. Henrik Ibsen is considered the Father of Modern Drama. How is *A Doll's House* different from any former plays?
4. Characterization- In drama, the characters tell the tale through their dialogue and actions. There must not be too many people on stage at any one time, for if the stage is too crowded, the audience may not be able to follow the action. In Greek Drama, for instance, each playwright was limited to three speaking actors. There is an unlimited number of nonspeaking, walk-on parts. Does this hold true for *A Doll's House* ?
5. Who or what is the Antagonist? Why?
6. Who or what is the Protagonist? Why?
7. An Archetype is an image, story pattern or character type which occurs frequently enough in literature to be recognizable. Name the archetype in this play. Explain.
8. Character Development- Tragedy must have some character growth. The protagonist learns from the tragedy inflicted upon him/her and becomes a more likable person. Explain the development seen in our protagonist.
9. Empathy- The audience must be able to identify with the characters to establish the dramatist's desired relationships. In a tragedy, for instance, the audience must feel sympathy for the major characters, for we must be emotionally affected by the fate of these characters if the play is to be successful. Explain to what extent this is true in *A Doll's House* .
10. Does *A Doll's House* have a Foil? Explain:
11. Dialogue is of vital importance to the success of a play. Aristotle wrote that what is said and how it is said are next in

importance to character, and if the dialogue is not accurate, the audience will not be able to follow the dramatist's ideas. Even the finest of writers of fiction are often unable to pen good dramatic dialogue. The quality of the dialogue, then, is the difference between bad and great plays. Quote one line that would be good or bad based on the above definition. Explain.

12. Theme- The main idea that the dramatist conveys to the audience is known as theme. Theme is the writer's view of the world or his revelation about human nature. What is the main theme of *A Doll's House* ?

13. Irony- This is a contrast or discrepancy between what is expected and what actually is. Situational Irony occurs when what actually happens is the opposite of the expected. Name one example of Situational Irony.

14. Dramatic Irony occurs when the audience knows something important that a character in the story or play does not know. Explain the significance of one example of Dramatic Irony.

Choose one of the following questions, using Ibsen's *A Doll's House* as evidence to complete the answer.

Question A:
Some novels and plays seem to advocate change in social or political attitudes or traditions. Note briefly the particular attitudes or traditions that Ibsen wants his 19th Century Victorian audience to change? Then explain how this would apply to today's society. Be sure to include the techniques Ibsen uses to influence the audience's views. Avoid plot summary.

Question B:
What would you say to someone to help him or her distinguish tragedy from pathos? Base your advice on *A Doll's House*.

Question C:
Select one to three scenes in *A Doll's House* that you felt was particularly moving. Compare the playwright's presentation of the respective scene(s), in relation to what you would expect the audience response to be.

Aristotle's Criteria for a Good Play

Tragedy is a type of drama in which the protagonist suffers disaster but in so doing attains heroic stature. Tragedy can be understoodbest by viewing it in terms of the original Greek concept described by Aristotle:

1. The plot must involve inner or outer conflict and some kind of decision. The main character must choose to perform or not to perform some morally meaningful act that will lead to the play's resolution.

2. The action must involve a noble person, who because of a "tragic flaw" makes a wrong decision which leads to an unhappy catastrophe.

3. The experience, although disastrous, deepens the hero's insight into his/her own nature and destiny.

4. Tragedy should have some catharsis. The desired effect should be a "purgation" of the emotions of pity and fear; that is, in feeling pity and fear for the tragic hero, the viewer's own tensions are released   and temporarily resolved.

Summary: The tragic hero whose character is marked by some tragic flaw, which is ultimately responsible for his downfall, moves us to pity, because his misfortune is greater than he deserves. It moves us to fear, because we recognize similar possibilities and consequences in our own fallible selves.

Aristotle's Definition of Tragedy

Aristotle defined tragedy as "an imitation of an action that is serious, complete, and of a certain magnitude; in language embellished with each kind of artful ornament, the several kinds being found in separate parts of the play, in the form of action, not of narration; through pity and fear affecting the proper purgation of these and similar emotions." To understand this definition, we must define each of the separate terms he used.:

Imitation means finding actions that are universal in that they would appeal to a large audience of various types of people and differing time periods.

Action means the decisions that must be made by the main characters and the ramifications that these decisions make.

Magnitude means that the characters and actions must rise above the ordinary. Although Aristotle's characters were either kings, gods, or great military leaders, Arthur Miller successfully challenged this notion in *Death of a Salesman* with the creation of Willy Loman, an ordinary tragic hero who was common to all of us.

Ornament includes diction and song. The diction (the way people talk) must be elevated. The songs or choral odes are sung in ritualistic and often complicated manners. Arthur Miller successfully challenged this too, having ordinary conversation as the basis for his play.

Purgation, or to use Aristotle's term, *catharsis*, means the feeling of being cleansed that an audience should have at the play's end. The tragic hero moves us to pity, because his misfortune is greater than he deserves. This moves us to fear, because we recognize similar possibilities in our own fallible selves.

The term tragedy does not mean a sad play with an unhappy ending. The point of all tragedy is that the protagonist, even though faced with impossible odds that will eventually cause his destruction, can rise above these odds. It is what he does that counts. A tragic hero will rise in courage and strength to display the godlike qualities that lie within each of us.

Thus, tragedy is not a depressing genre. It is positive and optimistic in its view of the possibilities of human potential. The tragic hero must be an individual who has greatness and a stature beyond the ordinary. Because of this, the audience experiences the catharsis referred to earlier when the tragic hero ultimately fails.

The tragic hero also has to have a "tragic flaw," such as overwhelming arrogance or pride, that leads to his downfall. This flaw could also be a poor choice that leads to his demise. The flaw could also be that he is too virtuous to exist in a world of ordinary beings. Regardless, the hero must be fully aware of what has happened to him in the end and must face that realization. He must proclaim his defiance, as Macbeth did in the end, and welcome his adversary.

There are two other terms to consider when discussing Aristotle's tragedy:

Peripeteia (also called *peripety*) occurs when an action produces the opposite of what was intended or expected. It is a reversal. Thus, Macbeth kills his king, Duncan, to gain happiness through power, put gains misery instead.

Anagnorisis means disclosure, discovery, or recognition. The tragic hero recognizes himself and his place.

Chapter SEVEN:

CREATIVE SUGGESTIONS

Literature and Composition AP

CREATIVE SUGGESTIONS-

Literature and Composition

AP students should be able to have fun too. The types of activities that follow are designed to encourage exploration, experimentation and FUN. As such, these are graded by the students themselves. I award ten points for every legitimate hour of work completed. I have my students fill out the chart on the following page when they are completed, and then we agree on a grade. They have a free choice of many activities; however, they must be prepared to share their end product with the class in an appropriate way.

One activity that I feel more and more is very important is memorizing. We teach them that words are powerful when arranged by the masters; we try to get them to emulate good writing. Why not have them memorize and recite good passages? Furthermore, the open question requires that they make apt and specific references to the work they've selected. Certainly, memorizing material from the longer works of literary merit assigned will help in the free choice essay.

Allowing this type of activity makes it fun for the teacher as well. These students are very gifted, and when given a bit of free rein, will pleasantly surprise everyone. The suggestions that follow are just that - suggestions. Students should be able to pick freely and modify the suggestions into an original project that best fits their talents.

Creativity for _____

(Name of Author)

Directions: Each student will select one creative project per author. Students will grade themselves. One hour's work earns a C. Two hour's work earns a B. Three hours work earns an A. One of these must be done for each author; however, if more than three hours are spent on one particular project, points may be banked and the next assignment reduced or waived. Eight hours total earns a creative grade of a C for the quarter. Ten hours total earns a creative grade of a B for the quarter. Twelve hours total earns a creative grade of a C for the quarter. Although freedom of choice is inherent in their creative projects, I make three hours of memorizing mandatory.

Name your creative project

_____

How many hours did you spend? _____

How many points did you earn? _____ How many points will be banked? _____

Summarize what you did:

Summarize what you learned:

What was you personal reaction to this assignment?

How will this information be useful to you now or in the future:

Jeopardy

Play the following game of Jeopardy or create one of your own. The following is a description of how the game of jeopardy can be modified to be used as a fun competition for a class.

The Procedure:

A. The class is divided into teams.

B. One team picks an answer from the grid.

C. The moderator reads the answer.

D. The team discusses the answer and the designated speaker of the group provides an answer within 20 seconds, or declines to answer.

E. The teacher acts as judge. If the answer is correct, the proper points are added. If answer is wrong, the points are subtracted. If the speaker declines to answer, no points are awarded or subtracted. This continues until the entire square is used.

F. In the final jeopardy round, the teacher tells each class what category is going to be used. The class will then wager X number of points. The teacher will read the answer and give them 30 seconds to respond. If the answer is right, they get the points wagered. If the answer is wrong, they lose the points. The team with the highest number of points at the end is the winner! Use the chart below to guide the game.

History	Poetry	Quotes	Authors	Myths	Isms
10	10	10	10	10	10
20	20	20	20	20	20
30	30	30	30	30	30
40	40	40	40	40	40
50	50	50	50	50	50

History

_____10. The nickname of the people who were led by Oliver Cromwell.

_____20. This man was the first Archbishop of Canterbury.

_____30. These two royal house were involved in the War of the Roses.

_____40. These are two of the three writers who were forerunners of the Romantic movement and lived during the last half of the 18th Century.

_____50. This author wrote through the eyes of his children from 1651 until his death in 1674.

Poetry

_____10. These three men were known as the Cavalier Poets.

_____20. In England's middle ages this title was given to any eminent poet.

_____30. This poet wrote "The Passionate Shepherd to his Love."

_____40. This English poet was known as the poet of the people and the poet of love.

_____50. This verse form contains lines of iambic pentameter without end rhyme.

Quotes

_____10. "In my younger and more vulnerable years, my father gave me some sound advice that I have been turning over in my mind ever since..." is from this character's thoughts.

_____20. "A little learning is a dangerous thing" was written by this essayist.

_____30. "The people say that the two seemed to be removed from human experience; that they had gone through pain and had come out on the other side; that there was almost a magical protection about them" is from this novel.

_____40. "Never fight fair with a stranger, boy. You'll never get out of the jungle that way" is from this literary work.

_____50. "Lawyers, I suppose, were children once" was written by this person .

Authors

_____10. This author wrote *The Iliad*.

_____20. This author wrote "The Pardoner's Tale."

_____30. This author, who is famous for modern tragedy, wrote *The Crucible*.

_____40. This Algerian author wrote about the rejection of God.

_____50. This author had his own cosmography of the world.

Mythology

_____10. This gift was sent to Epimetheus to his brother Prometheus.

_____20. This person was an admirer of a vain lad who was turned into a flower.

_____30. This daughter of Demeter causes the changing of seasons.

_____40. This man slayed Medusa.

_____50. This musician played his way into the Underworld to bring back his wife.

Isms

_____10. This ism paid tribute to the senses, emotions, and imagination.

_____20. This mid-nineteenth century Danish writer/philosopher was of the god of Theistic existentialists.

_____30. This ism believes that man is at the center of things.

_____40. These writers thought of art as communication rather than expression.

_____50. Mark Twain, Charles Dickens, George Eliot, Thomas Hardy, and Joseph Conrad produced works from this literary movement.

ANSWERS to JEOPARDY on page 120

Internet Activities: Locate, print, and read

1. Book reviews of the text assigned.

> A. Try to establish the credentials of the writer of the review. The reviews could be written by other high school students, other published authors, or the actual author.
> B. Examine the organization used by these writers? Do they have a clear thesis? Is their evidence specific? What makes the writing clear?

2. Selected passages of the text assigned.

3. A brief chronology of an author, poet, or playwright's life and other works written.

4. General criticism of the text.

5. Games created around texts assigned. One student found a game of jeopardy based on *The Great Gatsby.* The categories were IMAGES, TRANSFORMATION, NICK, GATSBY, NATURE OF TIME, FIVE LETTER WORDS, and FINAL JEOPARDY.

6. E-mail addresses: Write to authors of home pages . Respond to the information they have created.

7. Copy discussion made about a literary work on a "chat line."

8. Journal site: Many writers have their own Journal site.

9. Censorship: Find examples of a controversial work being banned by schools and libraries. For instance, the *San Francisco Chronicle*, May 29, 1885, wrote an article explaining why the Concord Public Library excluded Mark Twain's new book, *The Adventures of Huckleberry Finn.*

Other Creative Suggestions

1. Make a cover for your notes.

2. Draw a picture in response to what you read, or make a collage adding words from the text. Although many students are very artistic, very seldom are they given a chance with a reading assignment to express what they have comprehended through drawing.

3. Address letters to the speaker or main character of a work you are rereading.

4. List just the elements of plot as they occur in your epic poem, novel, short story, or play.

5. Find media pictures that seem to represent certain characters, setting, etc. Write a description of the character, setting, etc. beside the picture.

6. Copy quotations you find interesting. MEMORIZE THEM and recite to teacher. You will be expected to make apt and specific references to the text, so memorizing could help you score higher on the open question.

7. Make a vocabulary list of words used by the poet, author, playwright. Define the words.

8. Title chapters, scenes, stanzas, or rename titles.

9. Write a newspaper account of an episode.

10. Write examples of literary devices used by the writer: allusions, symbols, editorializing, imagery (the concrete verbal pictures that appeal to the senses), point of view (method of story telling), character description, length and rhythm of sentences, figurative language, dialogue (the colloquial phrases of the period), description, thematic statements, nature of time, form and structure, character growth.

11. Make a chart ("coded notes") showing how one basic element is advanced in the novel.
CHAPTER_____ CHARACTER OF _____

12. Copy well-written descriptions of the setting or of any of the basic elements of fiction.
> A. Write questions that help understand the passage.
> B. Write AP essay questions on attitude, literary elements, effect, or meaning.

13. Copy examples of two-word descriptions used in the work. For example: unrevealed capacity, breathless intensity, ripe mystery, scarcely withered, ravenously and unscrupulously, squeaked fashionably, safe and proud, etc.

14. Change general words into more descriptive words:
> FUN: engaging, stimulating, enjoyable, consuming, pleasurable, consuming, etc.
> OKAY: mediocre, marginal, acceptable, etc.
> ANGRY: furious, degrading, ranting, cross, affected, etc.

Try WENT, LITTLE, THINK, SAD, BAD, GOOD, EXAMPLE, DESCRIBE, USE, etc.

15. Update: What would the characters be doing now.

16. Make a list of three syllable words used by the writer.

17. List places most often mentioned in your longer work.

18. Note adjectives used by the writer to describe the main character's attitude: temperamental, curious, imaginative, smart, tempered, sensible, caring, adventurous, unique, well-educated, thoughtful, motherly, crabby, dreary, etc.

19. Write a newspaper obituary for a character in the text.

20. Write a book review of the text you are reading. Include the following topics:
> A. A statement of the general worth of the book. "The popular appeal of ____ lies in its ability to ____."
> B. A discussion of some of the elements that make the book recommended reading OR NOT.

21. Write down your response to the imagery of the work. Begin with: I see. . . I hear . . . I smell . . . I taste . . . I feel

22. Draw a comic strip version of an episode or do this on the computer as a slide show.

23. Make graffiti (drawings and writings normally scratched on walls) or a mural that illustrates concepts in the work read.

24. Describe the effectiveness of the narration. Was the narrator reliable, an effective communicator, unbiased, etc?

25. Find a poem, play, novel, or short story that relates to the one being read. Explain the relationship.

26. Make a drawing of a character as another character sees him/her.

27. Analyze your previous literary analysis papers by writing just the thesis and topic sentences. Change these so that each reveals a different insight on the same subject.

28. Describe a heroic decision made by a character in your novel, play, or poem.

29. Discuss the effectiveness of the work's ending.

30. Make any of the following additions to the text read:
> A. Add scenes that would alter the reader or audience's perception of the character.
> B. Make changes that would strengthen a weak character or weaken a strong character.
> C. Change relationships.
> D. Add editorialized comments to a scene to help illustrate thematic content.
> E. Make the characters's attitude more complex and ambiguous.
> F. Rewrite a scene in terms of being more "politically correct."

"Treasure Hunt" by Allissa Kovala

Directions:

1. Divide into eight groups of two or three students.

2. Read the first clue in class. Everyone has the same starting clue.

3. Locate the envelope somewhere in the school building with the first sets of clues.

4. Find the sheet with your group number.

5. Read the next clue for your group (each group has the same clues, but in a different order).

6. Locate the next envelope. Write down the order you followed to get back to the English classroom.

7. The first group back wins a small package of gum.

Here are the clues. The answers are provided, but they would obviously be omitted for the competition.

    A. Jay Gatsby had one of these in his back yard:
        _____ (Pool)

    B. " . . . Had nothing to fear but fear itself." I read this quote from *To Kill a Mockingbird* in this class (not English Language and Composition!) ___(US History)

    C. Myrtle was killed by a car driven by Daisy. Daisy would have learned in _____ that she should have stopped after she killed Myrtle. (Driver's Ed)

    D. Atticus could play the Jew's Harp in this room.
        _____ (Band)

    E. Scout was dressed as a ham when she was on the _____ (Stage)

    F. Walter Cunningham should have gone here to treat his cooties. _____ (Nurse's Office)

    G. Huck had a friend named this. _____(Gym)

    H. Huck needed a saw to cut a hole in the cabin wall. You'll find one of these in the _____ (Shop)

    I. Scout would always talk to Calpurnia here:
        _____ (Kitchen - Home Ec "Laker Shake Shoppe")

    J. We read the books *To Kill a Mockingbird, The Great Gatsby, The Adventures of Huckleberry Finn,* and *The Scarlet Letter* in this class: _____ (American Masters-AP)

Poetry

1. Think of a common English word that would be an example of each of the type of feet:

      A. Iamb (short / long)-

      B. Trochee (long / short)-

      C. Spondee (long / long)-

      E. Anapest (short / short / long)-

      F. Dactyl (long / short / short)-

      G. Amphibrach (short / long / short)-

      H. Amphimacer (long / short / long)-

2. Scan your own first and last name. Name its meter by stating its type of foot first and the number of feet next.

      A. Name-

      B. Type of foot-

      C. Number of feet-

3. Scan the first and last names of ten other class members. Name their meter by stating their type of foot first and the number of feet next.

      A.
      B.
      C.
      D.
      E.
      F.
      G.
      H.
      I.
      J.

Computer Game
by Birk Larsen and Nate Swanberg

Name of Project: Big Huck

Hours Spent on Project: About 15-20 Hours Each

Points Earned: 120

Points Banked: 0

Summarize What You Did:

Nate and I created a computer game using many applications on the computer. It was modeled after a game that we first saw in about ninth grade that had Bill Clinton called "Slick Willie." There is some general information for the game that should be known to help make sense of the game.

1. All of the gray characters moving on the screen are the Statue of Liberty. This is a metaphor for American freedom. Huck must eat all of them (by moving your mouse) to move on to the next of 11 continually cycling   levels.

2. Bonus Items include a Ham, a Raft, and a 50 cent Gold Coin. These items are all worth 50 points if Huck eats them. The ham is a symbol for the search of food. The raft floats by to help Huck get his and Jem's freedom. The gold piece is for Huck to buy necessities.

3. You must avoid all of the bad things:
   a. Pap dripping blood and flashing (because of Huck's escape).
   b. The St. Petersburg times (the newspaper from Huck's town).
   c. A Bloody Knife (the one that Huck used to kill the pig).
   d. A Flaming Building (Jim's shed after the farmers "busted in").

    e. Hitler's Head (a metaphor for hatred and racism).

    f. The police badge (he must avoid the law).

    g. The Skull (a symbol for superstition).

    h. Tom Sawyer (so Huck does not get caught).

Summarize What You Learned:

We learned how to better use the computer, how to create metaphors, how to interpret metaphors, and how to have fun on a long assignment.

Reaction To This Assignment: We enjoyed working with the computer and being able to create this game.

How Will This Information Be Useful To You In The Future:

We have a better understanding of personal and general metaphors and symbols. We also explored different programs and learned how to use them better.

ACADEMY AWARDS

In the fall, I teach a class called American Masters to Advanced Placement students. One of the goals of the class is to write comparison and contrast papers, selecting two or three of the major longer works of literary merit assigned. To help them find a "common ground" among these works as a starting point for a topic, I have them vote for their choice of the following categories. Discussing the nominations and selecting a winner provides many examples of common elements.

Superior Category:

1. Best Supporting Actor:

2. Best Supporting Actress:

3. Most Interesting (complex, amusing, most loved) character:

4. Best Author:

Why?

5. Best Story Line (Explain):

6. Best Theme (Name it):

7. Most Dramatic Scene (Name it):

8. The Funniest Line:

9. The Best Title:

10. The Most Mysterious Character:

11. The Best Conflict:

12. The Best Couple:

Wretched Category:

1. The Character I Most Loved to Hate:

2. Reject Award (The Book Most Wanted to Throw Away):

3. The Most Empty-headed Theme:

4. The Worst Character (Least Well-Rounded):

5. The Worst Author:

6. The Worst Story-line:

7. The Worst Couple:

8. The Worst Title:

9. The "I Wouldn't Send a Postcard from this Setting" Award:

10. The Most Boring Scene:

Creative Suggestions for Poetry

Make groups of five words or more for each of the following categories:

1. Riming -

2. Alliteration -

3. Assonance -

4. Synonyms - Other?   (100 words are needed.)

5. Every Time is Rhyme Time

> A. Compose original sentences with internal rhyme. Each sentence must have four words that rhyme.   Fifteen sentences must be completed.
> B. Examples:
> > 1. "The rain in Spain falls mainly in the plain."
> > 2. "Rubble and stubble make double trouble."

6. Create a Poetry Collage - an artistic composition of fragments of materials pasted on a picture surface.

> 1. This collage should contain a partial or complete definition of poetry.

> 2. This collage should contain a poem or parts of poetry to illustrate that definition.

> 3. The poetry must be typed, printed, or in some other neat, legible, readable manner displayed on the college.

> 4. The collage should be larger than regular sized paper unless a particular artistic shape is used.

> 5. Paper suggested would be construction, tag board, etc.

> 6. The collage should be proper for display purposes.

ART OPTIONS

1. Make a scarecrow image of a character. Make a cross out of two 1X1 boards. Attach to a 2X4 base. Cut a circle out of cardboard. Draw a face on the circle and attach it as the head. Clothe the crossed boards in baby clothing. Add hair or hat to make it more authentic.

2. Make a plywood poster. Cut a thin plywood board down to a 3' X 3' size. Paint the background white. Draw and paint colored version of the title of the text being illustrated. Add painted symbols to surround the title.

3. Make Leggo constructions that would represent symbols, settings, characters, etc. in your text.

4. Decorate an old three-bladed fan to illustrate relationships. For instance, place a symbol of a main character in the middle. The decorate each blade with concerns, topic, themes, other characters, etc. that are related to the main character symbolized in the middle of the fan.

5. Construct a setting on a small plywood base. Include buildings, vegetation, roads, etc.

6. Draw a caricature of a character in a text.

7. Make a humorous, condensed version of some of the longer works of fiction you have been assigned to read. Example:
> A. *Moby Dick:* Ahab chases whale. Whale chases Ahab. Whale prevails.
> B. *Romeo & Juliet:* Two teenagers fall in love and then they die.
> C. *Gone with the Wind:* Scarlet's a yuppie. The South falls. Rhett splits.
> D. *A Tale of Two Cities:* Good times. Bad times. The peasants win. Marie loses.
> E. *War and Peace:* A lot of Russians with long names doing complicated things. The Czars lose.
> *Anonymous*

ANSWERS to JEOPARDY:

History

10. What were the Roundheads?

20. Who was St. Augustine?

30. Who were The House of Lancaster and the House of New York?

40. Who were Thomas Gray, Robert Burns, William Blake?

50. Who is Milton?

Poetry

10. Who were Herrick, Lovelace and Suckling?

20. What is a Poet Laureate?

30. Who was Christopher Marlowe?

40. Who was Robert Burns?

50. What is blank verse?

Quotes

10. Who is Nick Carraway, the narrator of *The Great Gatsby*?

20. Who was Alexander Pope?

30. What is *The Pearl* ?

40. What is *Death of a Salesman*?

50. Who is Charles Lamb?

Authors

10. Who is Homer?

20. Who is Geoffery Chaucer?

30. Who is Arthur Miller?

40. Who is Camus?

50. Who is Milton?

Mythology

10. What is Pandora's box?

20. Who was Echo?

30. Who is Persephone?

40. Who is Perseus?

50. Who is Eurydice?

Isms

10. What is Romanticism?

20. Who was Kierkegaard?

30. What is humanism?

40. What are the Neoclassicists?

50. What are the Realists?

Chapter Eight:

Writing Prompts

Literature and Composition AP

Writing Prompts- Literature and Composition

AP students need practice writing in three different ways:

A. Extended writing
B. Free writing
C. Forty minute writing

"Extended writing" is that in which the writer works on a longer piece of writing over an extended period of time. All aspects of the writing process are developed: selection of topic, brainstorming, collecting specific evidence, writing drafts, revising, editing, and finishing the piece. Doing all this over an extended period of time allows the student "rest time" to forget the writing and then revisit it later for fresh perspectives. Doing this over an extended period of time allows for more thoughtful reflection on the topic. Doing this over a period of time allows for better struggles over word choice and syntax that is so important to developing more effective writing.

"Free writing" is a shorter, varied type of writing that allows the student to explore and experiment with his or her own writing style. This should be done daily, or at least frequently. Examples that follow are just suggestions. Students should use these as a starting point, developing their own topics as the occasion arises.

"Forty minute writing" is the writing unique to the AP test. Students need to practice this on their own as formal, teacher-assigned tasks. Some of these should be graded using the checklists in chapter two, and some should not.

Extended Writing Assignment One

Write a 700-1,000 word paper throughout the quarter following the directions below:

A. The method of approach and format of the assignment will be at the discretion of the student. For example, you may choose from any of the following:

1. Analysis of a key passage
2. Comparison of two key passages.
3. Commentary on a key passage or a whole work.
4. Other?

B. Each candidate should choose ONE of the following.

1. A detailed appreciation of an aspect on ONE work studied in which you

a. Demonstrate an understanding of the aspect chosen (e.g. genre, period, theme, type of literary study).
b. Indicate evidence of careful reading of the work

OR

2. A comparative study of an aspect of two works. You may select from the works listed below or choose two other appropriate works:

Miller's *The Crucible*
Shakespeare's *Hamlet*
T. S. Eliot and his contemporaries
Nathaniel Hawthorne's works
Williams' *A Streetcar Named Desire*
O'Neill's *The Emperor Jones*
Euripedes' *Medea*
Twain's *The Adventures of Huckleberry Finn*
Lee's *To Kill a Mockingbird*
Dostoevsky's *Crime and Punishment*
Fitzgerald's *The Great Gatsby*

Note: The two works should be chosen for similarity of genre, period, theme, type of literary study, and methodology. The assignment should:

a. Demonstrate an understanding of the aspect chosen.
b. Indicate evidence of careful reading of the TWO texts.

A Second Quarter-Long Assignment

Write a 1,000 - 1,500 word paper throughout the quarter following the directions below:

> A. The student's study will be based on three works of his or her choice, but approved by the teacher.

> B. The student will choose the three works based on a similar aspect or a similar theme.

> C. The aspect may reflect the interests of the student and the underlying approach to the works studied.
> > EXAMPLES:
> > 1. Narrative Technique
> > 2. Characterization
> > 3. Portrayal of society in the literature studied
> > 4. Universal perspective of common human problems
> > 5. Universal perspective of portrayal of the family

> D. The piece of work need not, necessarily, be in the form of a formal essay, but it must be a developed piece of writing.

> E. Content and format guidelines:
> > INTRODUCTION:
> > 1. The works which have been read
> > 2. The reason for the choice of the aspect
> > 3. The direction the study of the aspect has taken
> > CORE:
> > Substantiation of what the candidate set out to do, using specific examples from the three works
> > CONCLUSION:
> > The candidates personal evaluation of the study and the conclusions reached

Free Writing

1. Explain the choices that would be included in a rewriting of a passage in a more modern, or more Classical, or more Romantic style.

2. Review a scene in one of the plays you read. Write an interior monologue showing how the scene would change if we heard what a minor character is thinking.

3. Have a character from a text write a diary or journal entry.

4. Show how a passage would change if another writer previously studied would have written a scene from the play or story.

5. Have one writer question another on a character in another writer's text.

6. Show some original research which is helpful in understanding the text.

7. Write a paper on the sensations elicited by the writer through his or her use of imagery. Comment on the writer's effectiveness or connection to other details in writing (Cite Page).

8. Write a paper on style by copying passages that strike you as well-written and comment on their effectiveness .

9. Be a reporter and write a newspaper account of a dramatic scene in one of the novels. Remember the journalist's formula: tell who, what, when, where, why. Question two or three witnesses who were present in this scene.

10. Make the story into a movie by writing the script. Pick the scenes that would be best selected and explain why.

11. From the viewpoint of helping or hurting someone else's personality or character, compare one of the characters in one of the novels to any other character you have read or seen in a movie.

12. Write an editorial on the death of one of the characters in

one of the novels, short stories, plays or poems read, as a reporter who happened to see the incident.

13. Write a horoscope reflecting various scenes or themes in any of the books.

14. Write a want ads page reflecting concerns of people in the time period of a particular novel.

15. Write a diary entry reflecting a day in the life of one of the characters in the story.

16. Write a news brief explaining a dramatic scene in the story.

17. Write the script for a "Talk Show" interview with an author and/or some of the fictional characters in his book.

18. WRITE POETRY

Forty Minute Essay Writing

1. Identify the author's attitude toward what he or she is describing. Explain how this perspective shapes the way the writer presents the material.

2. Write a Literature "Open" Question, selecting ideas from the content of the following or select your own.

    A. Choose a work in which the title has significance and show how the meaning of the title is revealed implicitly through the author's use of such devices as contrast, repetition, and allusion.

    B. Choose a novel or play in which the opening chapter or scene is important in revealing the various themes that are important to the overall work.

    C. Choose a novel or play in which the ending doesn't end, but rather requires the reader to adjust to some ambiguity or uncertainty. Discuss the appropriateness or inappropriateness of this particular type of ending.

D. Choose a novel or play of literary merit written before 1900 and discuss its relevance to today's society.

E. Choose a novel or a play in which a minor character plays a major role in the story, perhaps by affecting the plot in a unique way, or perhaps by critically affecting the role of the major character by acting as a foil or a confidante.

F. Choose a novel or play in which the full presentation of the villain creates some reader sympathy for his plight.

3. Analyze poetry or passages writing your own questions to guide you. Use the typical questions in Chapter Two as models for your own questions.

4. Find similar poetry or prose passages. Write a comparison and contrast essay in which you discuss their similarities and differences.

5. Write essays on previously given AP exams.

6. Write an essay that compares two different translations of the same novel, Albert Camus' *The Stranger,* for instance.

Chapter Nine

Glossary of Terms

Literature and Composition AP

Glossary of Terms

used in the 1970 — 1997 (AP) Advanced Placement
Examinations in

Literature and Composition

- **Abstraction**

    A concept or value that can not be seen (love, honor,
    courage, etc.) which the writer usually tries to illus-
    trate by comparing it metaphorically to a known, con-
    crete object. Sometimes this knowledge is hidden or
    esoteric because it is only known by or meant for a
    select few.

- **Allegory**

    A story or description that has a second meaning. This
    is portrayed by creating characters, setting, and/or
    events which represent (symbolize) abstract ideas.

- **Alliteration**

    The repetition at close intervals of initial consonant
    sounds.

- **Allusion**

    References to literary, artistic, scientific, or historical
    people, places, or things by the author to convey tone,
    purpose, or effect.

- **Ambiguity**

    The expression of an idea in such a way that more than
    one meaning is suggested. All AP essay passages have
    some ambiguity. To get the highest scores, students
    have to make reference to the multiple meanings seen
    in the passages.

- **Analogy**

    A comparison of two things usually made by an au-
    thor to show how something unfamiliar is like some-
    thing widely known. In an essay, if you are not sure if
    it is a metaphor or a simile, call it an analogy.

- **Anapest**

    A metrical foot that has two unstressed syllables fol-
    lowed by one stressed syllable.

- **Anecdote**

  A brief story used in an essay to illustrate a point.

- **Antagonist**

  The force or person working against the protagonist. The villain is an antagonist.

- **Antithesis**

  A contrast of ideas expressed in a grammatically balanced statement. "To err is human; to forgive, divine."

- **Antecedent**

  The noun for which the pronoun stands.

- **Aphorism**

  A brief, sometimes clever saying that expresses a principle, truth or observation about life (see assertion).

- **Apostrophe**

  A literary device in which the speaker directly addresses someone dead, someone missing, an abstract quality, or something nonhuman as if he/she/it were present. Example" "Ye knew him well, ye cliffs."

- **Approximate Rhyme**

  Using words that have some sound correspondence, but the rhyme is not perfect.

- **Aside**

  Private words, spoken by an actor to the audience, that are not meant to be heard by other characters in the play.

- **Assertion**

  A categorical statement made by the author, speaker, narrator, or character which generalizes an opinion usually about human nature.

- **Attitude**

  The author's state of mind or point of view toward himself/herself or another person, place, or thing.

- **Ballad Meter**

  A ballad is a fairly short story or poem that has some songlike qualities. A typical ballad stanza is a quatrain with the rhyme scheme abcb. The meter is primarily iambic.

- **Blank Verse**

  Poetry written in unrhymed iambic pentameter.

- **Characterization**

  The process by which the writer reveals the personalities of the people of the work. This can be done in the following ways:

1. Direct author/poet statement: The author may use such direct diction as "cruel, conservative, deceitful, long-suffering," or "self-absorbed"

2. Motivations: Some examples could include misguided altruisms, self-destructive ambition, self-conscious insecurity, financial considerations, or hypocritical tendencies.

3. Physical Description

4. Dialogue

5. Thoughts and feelings

6. Actions

7. Effect on others, etc.

•**Closed Couplet**

Two consecutive lines of poetry that rhyme and present a completed thought.

•**Comic Relief**

Something said or done that provides a break from the seriousness of the story, poem, or play.

•**Comparison and Contrast**

Showing similarities and/or differences. The AP question usually asks for differences. The student is asked to make a judgment about the relative merits of the two passages. Which one is more effective?

•**Conceit**

A juxtaposition that makes a surprising connection between two seemingly different things. T. S. Eliot is a modern poet known for his use of conceits.

•**Conclusion**

Usually written to reaffirm or finally state the thesis. Other strategies used in the conclusion include expressing a final thought about a subject, summarizing main points, using a quotation, predicting an outcome, making an evaluation, or recommending a course of action.

•**Confessional Poetry**

A modern term used to describe poetry that uses intimate and usually painful, disturbing, or sad material from the poet's life. Anne Sexton and Sylvia Plath are two modern Confessional poets.

•**Conflict**

The tension created in the story by the struggle or

outcome of the struggle — one of the narrative devices to address when analyzing the tone of the passage. Look for internal, as well as external conflict.

•**Connotative Language**

Words which have implied meaning, emphasizing the feelings or subjectivity that surrounds the word. Denotative language, emphasizing the literal, dictionary meaning, is used to create an objective tone. Consider these aspects of words when analyzing how diction creates attitude, effect, or purpose.

•**Contrast**

A literary technique in which the author examines two opposites (like the energy of youth and the infirmity of age, worldly possessions and democratic idealism, academic success and extracurricular activities, a speaker's sophistication and the student's naivete, or a group's smug views and the speaker's implied disapproval of them) to create an attitude, accomplish a purpose of effect, or to make an assertion.

•**Control a wide range of the elements of writing**

In mature writing, mature diction, varied syntax and effective paragraph organization combine to convey a clear and insightful evaluation, analysis, impression, or assertion.

•**Dactyl**

A metrical foot with one stressed syllable followed by two unstressed syllables.

•**Deduction**

The act of drawing a conclusion from known facts or general principles. An typical AP multiple choice question may be "Which of the following is a logical deduction from the speaker's assertions?"

•**Definition**

One means of organizing writing. For example, an abstract idea may be developed with a number of definitions of the idea.

•**Denotative Language**

Denotative words have literal, dictionary meaning, emphasizing an objective tone. Connotative language has implied meaning, emphasizing the feelings or subjectivity that surrounds the word. Consider these aspects of words when analyzing how diction creates attitude, effect, or purpose.

- **Description**

    Using vivid words to paint a picture of what the five senses are experiencing. The purpose of a descriptive essay is to create a **dominant impression** through a manipulation of details.

- **Diction**

    Word choice used by the author to persuade or to convey tone, purpose, or effect.

- **Dialogue**

    Conversation between people.

- **Didactic**

    Type of writing that is preachy or bossy.

- **Dilemma**

    A type of conflict in which both choices have some negative connotations.

- **Dramatic Monologue**

    A poem in which the speaker addresses one or more listeners who remain silent or whose replies are not revealed.

- **Dramatize**

    To act.

- **Economy**

    A style of writing characterized by conciseness and brevity.

- **Effect**

    The influence or result of something, using such rhetorical strategies as arguments, assumptions, attitudes, contrast, diction, imagery, pacing, or repetition. This effect could include such results as to intensify the speaker's sense of the ridiculous, reveal the speaker's ___ attitude, emphasize the cynicism of ___, reduce ___ to the level of low comic characters, or to glamorize a character.

- **End-stopped Lines**

    Lines of poetry that end with punctuation marks.

- **Epigram**

    A short, witty statement, often with a clever twist of thought. An example would be "Experience is the name everyone gives to his mistakes." Certain lines of poetry could have an epigrammatic effect.

- **Euphemism**

    Describing something distasteful in a positive way.

•Euphony

> A choice and arrangement of words that creates a pleasant sound.

•Exposition

> One of four major forms of writing, in which explanations are set forth. The other three types of discourse are called narrative, descriptive, and persuasive.

•Extended Figure

> Any metaphor, simile, personification, or apostrophe that is developed through several lines or throughout the poem.

•Feelings

> One purpose of a poem may be to convey a feeling of curiosity, contentment, remoteness, resignation, or foreboding.

•Foreshadowing

> A literary technique in which the author gives hints about future events.

•Figures of Speech

> Imaginative comparisons (similes, metaphors, personification, etc.) used by the author to convey tone, purpose, or effect.

•Foil

> A character who contrasts with another character.

•Foot

> A unit of meter that contains an arranged numbered of syllables. For instance, an anapest foot contains two unstressed syllables followed by one stressed syllable. Other types of feet are called dactyl, iamb, spondee, and trochee.

•Form

> An AP essay may ask how the writer uses form to accomplish a purpose or create an attitude or effect. Form is the external pattern of the poem. Different types of form include: continuous form (lines follow each other without formal grouping, breaking only at the end of a unit of meaning), stanzaic form, free verse, fixed form (the ballad, Terza Rima, etc.) and blank verse.

•Flashback

> One aspect of narrative structure in which the writer goes back in time to reveal past history that is somehow important to the story.

•**Foreshadowing**

> Another aspect of narrative structure in which the author maintains interest by giving clues about future happenings.

•**Free Verse**

> Poetry that does not conform to a regular pattern of rhyme or rhythm. The words are arranged in lines but have no fixed meter.

•**Grotesque**

> An element of Gothic Romanticism in which bizarre, fantastically ugly or absurd elements are somehow important to the overall effect of the poem or story.

•**Heroic Couplet**

> Two consecutive lines of poetry that rhyme and are written in iambic pentameter.

•**Hyperbole**

> A figure of speech in which the author uses overexaggeration or overstatement to create a certain effect, accomplish a particular purpose or reveal an attitude.

•**Iamb**

> A metrical foot that has one unaccented syllable followed by one accented syllable.

•**Imagery**

> Diction describing the senses (visual, tactile, auditory, olfactory, etc.) used by the author to convey tone, purpose, or effect.

•**Internal Rhyme**

> Rhyme that occurs within a line of poetry. Example: "The fair breeze blew, the white foam flew."

•**Inverted Order**

> Reversing the normal subject-verb-complement order seen in a sentence. Poets sometimes change this order to conform to rhyme and rhythm patterns. Prose writers may change this order for emphasis.

•**Irony**

> A literary device used by authors, playwrights, and poets in which the writer implies a discrepancy between what is said and what is meant (verbal irony), between what happens and what is expected to happen (situational irony), or between what a character in a play thinks and what the audience knows to be true (dramatic irony).

•**Juxtaposition**

> Placing two unlike persons, places or things next to each other to create an effect, reveal an attitude, or accomplish a purpose. Such juxtaposition could include a married couple, two types of religions, or such abstract ideas as virtue and youth, innocence and egotism, or wealth and poverty.

•**Litotes**

> See understatement.

•**Lyrical Poetry**

> A poem whose main purpose is to express the personal feelings or thoughts of the speaker rather than to tell a story.

•**Manipulation of Language**

> A skillful handling of diction and syntax used by the author to convey tone, purpose, or effect.

•**Metaphysical Conceit (see Conceit)**

> So-called because they were used by the Metaphysical Poets of the seventeenth century. This type of conceit is especially startling, complex and ingenious.

•**Metaphor**

> A direct comparison in which an unknown item is understood by directly comparing it to a known item Metaphors can be **directly stated** or **implied**. When it is developed throughout the poem or over several lines, it is called an **extended metaphor.** One that has been used too often is called a **dead metaphor**, and one that compares things that are visually or imaginatively incompatible is called a **mixed metaphor.**

•**Meter**

> A set of stressed and unstressed syllables of a poetic line, carefully counted to conform to a regular pattern. Meter is described by the type of foot used (iambic, trochaic, dactylic, or anapestic) and the number of feet in each line (monometer, dimeter, trimeter, tetrameter, pentameter, hexameter, heptameter, or octometer). **Blank verse** is written in iambic pentameter because each foot has an unstressed syllable followed by a stressed syllable, and each line has five of these iambic feet.

- **Narrative Structure or Narrative Techniques**

  A chronology of events, plot, conflict, characterization, setting, and other elements of story telling to convey tone, purpose, or effect.

- **Narrator (Also called Point of View)**

  The person telling the story. This person can be described as a participating observer who is partial to someone, a third person narrator who is aware of the main character's thoughts (central omniscient), a non-participating narrator who is unaware of the main character's thoughts (third person objective), a first person narrator who refers of himself in the third person, a third person narrator who reveals the thoughts of several characters (Omniscient).

- **Naturalism**

  A nineteenth-century literary movement that carried realism to a negative extreme. In naturalistic stories character outcomes are doomed by heredity and environment.

- **Octave**

  An eight line poem, or the first eight lines of a Petrarchan sonnet.

- **One - Side - At - A - Time Method**

  One of two ways to organize a comparison-contrast essay. In this type of organization the writer would discuss all the points of one passage first, then discuss all the points of the other passage second, showing the differences between the two. This technique may also be called the "Block Method."

- **Onomatopoeia**

  The use of words that imitate the sound that the word makes (buzz).

- **Organization**

  The process of arranging evidence to support a thesis. This organizational choice could be chronological, spatial, emphatic, simple to complex, definition, cause and effect, deductive, inductive, comparison and contrast, division and classification, examples, analogy, side-by-side, point-by-point, etc.

- **Oxymoron**

  A figure of speech that combines contradictory terms (cheerfully vindictive, jumbo shrimp, deafening silence, the living dead).

- **Pacing** - The rate of movement (tempo) of a story. Pacing may be slower with exposition or description, faster with dramatic incidence, etc.
- **Paradigm**
  A model, ideal or standard.
- **Parallel Structures**
  A stylistic technique in which items in a series are created with identical grammatical structures.
- **Paradox**
  A statement or situation that appears contradictory but is true. For instance, the mountains in a setting of a poem may be both remote and oppressively present. Metaphysical and Cavalier poets of the 17th century made great use of paradoxes.
- **Paraphrase**
  To restate the content of the poem in prose.
- **Parody**
  A rewriting of a popularly recognized work to make fun of something. Rewriting *Little Red Riding Hood* in more "politically correct" language would be an example of a parody.
- **Petrarchan or Italian Sonnet**
  A 14 line poem organized in two segments: the octave (the first 8 lines) with the rhyme scheme *abbaabba* and a sestet (the last six lines with the rhyme scheme *cdecde* or *cdcdcd*. The other type of Sonnet is called an Elizabethan or Shakespearean Sonnet.
- **Personification**
  A figure of speech in which inanimate objects are given human qualities (The fog comes in on little cat feet).
- **Persuasion**
  Writing which appeals to the reader's emotions and value systems, encouraging the reader to adopt an attitude or change a position.
- **Plausibility**
  An element of literary judgment. Is the work Believable? Whether the work is Romantic or Realistic, some element of believability must exist for reader empathy to occur.

- **Point - by - point -**

    One of two ways to organize a comparison-contrast essay. In this type of organization, the writer would discuss one aspect of both passages, showing how this one aspect differs; then the writer would do the same for a second and possibly third aspect, intertwining evidence from both passages in each paragraph.

- **Point of View**

    The tone or attitude created by the author's manipulation of language. ALSO SEE NARRATOR.

- **Pun**

    A play upon words based on the multiple meanings of words. Puns are usually used to create humor, but can be a serious element in poetry as well.

- **Purpose**

    The reason for writing an essay, usually based on the effect the writer wants to have on his/her audience.

- **Quatrain**

    A poem of four lines, or a stanza of four lines within a poem.

- **Realism**

    A literary style developed in the nineteenth century that attempts to portray life accurately without idealizing or romanticizing it.

- **Refrain**

    A repeated word, phrase, or group of lines in poetry.

- **Relevance**

    A question of pertinence. How does a work of literary merit written before 1900 relate to modern reader.

- **Repetition**

    A device used by the writer to emphasize an important character trait, to reinforce the story's theme, to highlight the speaker's attitude, etc.

- **Resolution**

    The conclusion of the story.

- **Rhetorical Purpose**

    The reason for the speaker's remarks; or a definition of the attitude that the author would like the reader to adopt.

- **Rhetorical Structure**

    Any organizational device used by the author to convey tone, purpose, or effect. Such writing choices may include establishing a thesis, presenting a description, presenting a contrasting description, describing an expectation, posing a question and answering it, beginning a narrative and embellishing it, etc.

•Rhetorical Strategy

Writing choices made by the author to accomplish purpose. These may include such things as allowing the reader to form individual judgments, undercutting the speaker's statements with irony, imitating the language of a certain group of people, beginning and ending on a note of uncertainty, or contrasting the setting and its inhabitants. Rhetorical innovation is a mark of good writing.

•Rhetorical Shift

A change in attitude, purpose, or effect seen in a literary work For example, a speaker's mode of expression may change from one of criticism to acceptance, homage to entreaty, rationality to enthusiasm, uncertainty to resolution, or languor to determination. The shift may also be more structural, such as a digression from the main subject of the poem, a change from description to narration, a counterargument to establish the speaker's credibility, metaphorical application of an image in the poem, or a simile for the relationship between two characters.

•Rhetorical Question

A literary device in which a question is asked that actually requires no answer.

•Rime Royal

A Chaucerian Stanza composed of seven lines written in iambic pentameter with a rhyme scheme of ababbcc.

•Romanticism

A literary movement that emphasizes intuition, imagination, and emotions over reason. Most romantics are outspoken in their love of nature and contempt for material things. Most romantics are concerned with the ideal rather than the real. An AP essay may ask you to address romantic diction or romantic atmosphere.

- **Satire**

  A type of writing which makes fun of human weakness, vice, or folly in order to bring about change. Some ways to satirize include mingling the serious and the trivial indiscriminately, juxtaposing religious and political views, using repetition to exaggerate character weakness, vice, or folly, etc.

- **Selection and Presentation of Specific Detail**

  Facts, circumstances, characteristics, techniques, etc., used by the author to convey tone, purpose, or effect.

- **Sestet**

  Six lines of poetry, especially the last six lines of a Petrarchan sonnet.

- **Setting**

  The time and location of the story. The setting may be used by the writer to create conflict, atmosphere, mood, or character.

- **Shakespearean Sonnet**

  A 14 line poem composed of three quatrains, followed by a rhyming couplet. The rhyme scheme is abab, cdcd, efef, gg.

- **Soliloquy**

  A long speech made by a character in a play while he/she is alone on stage.

- **Sound**

  An element to consider when analyzing poetry. For instance, an alliteration for the "s" sound may be appropriate for a poem about the ocean.

- **Spenserian Stanza**

  A nine line stanza with the rhyme scheme ababbcbcc. The first eight lines are written in iambic pentameter and the last line is **alexandrine** - iambic hexameter. This form was created by Edmond Spenser and used by such poets as John Keats, Percy Byssche Shelly, Lord Byron, and Robert Burns.

- **Symbol**

  A person, place or thing that represents something else . . . for instance, the whippoorwill in the poem could be presented as a symbol of death. . . a cross could be a symbol of the villager's plight, etc.

- **Syntax (Sentence Structure)**

    The arrangement of words into sentences used by the author to convey tone, purpose, or effect. These can be described as simple, compound, or complex; argumentative, expository, interpretive or narrative; declarative, imperative, interrogative, or exclamatory.

- **Terza Rima**

    An interlocking, three line stanza form with the rhyme scheme aba bcb cdc ded, etc.

- **Theme**

    The central idea, usually by the writer of a work. Theme deals with the writer's view of the world which implicitly reveals some insight about human nature. A good way to start to define theme is to determine the subject of the work. Some subjects could include religious skepticism, emotional deprivation, hopeless deprivation, excessive wildness, or excessive wealth. A description of the passage and its general theme may include such elements as a character analysis of two professional people which emphasizes the elements of idealism and selflessness that motivate them, or a narrative treatment of the conflicts inherent in the structure of social classes; etc.

- **Tone -**

    The attitude created by the author's manipulation of language. AP passages dealing with tone are complex and ambiguous. To achieve the highest marks on tone essays, the writer has to define the tone in a specifically complex way. Some examples would include: bitterness tempered with maturity, respect strengthened by distance, servility imparted by discipline, perplexity compounded by resentment, or gratitude made richer by love.

- **Total Meaning**

    The entire experience communicated by the poem: sensuous, emotional, intellectual, imaginative, etc.

- **Tragedy**

    A play in which the protagonist comes to an unhappy end. The main character is usually an honorable person whose downfall is caused by what Aristotle called a **tragic flaw** (an error in judgment or character weakness).

•Transcendentalism

> A nineteenth century movement in the Romantic tradition which believes that humans can rise above materialism to a higher happiness through simplicity and communion with nature.

•Understatement (Litotes)

> A statement that says less than what it means. These are often used to make an ironic point.

•Wit

> A quality of writing that combines cleverness with keen perception, especially in the writer's ability to state things that the reader has thought but not been able to express in words.

-

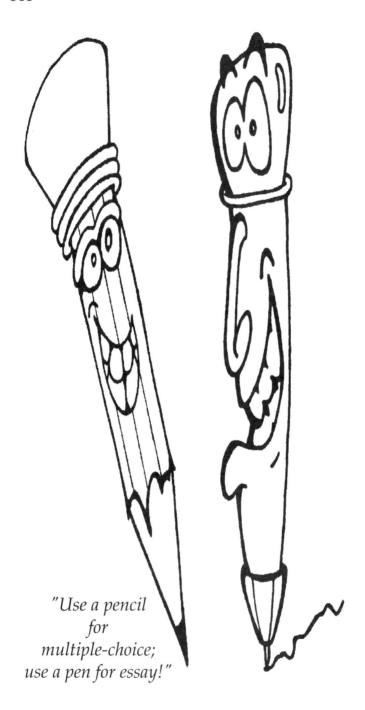

"Use a pencil
for
multiple-choice;
use a pen for essay!"

Chapter Ten: Practice Tests

Literature and Composition AP

Practice Test 1:

Section 1
Multiple-
Choice

ENGLISH LITERATURE
AND COMPOSITION
    SECTION I - Time -- 1 class period
Directions: This part consists of selections from prose works
and questions on their content, form, and style. After reading
each passage, choose the best answer to each question and completely fill in the corresponding oval on the answer sheet.
Note: Pay particular attention to the requirement of the questions that contain the words NOT, LEAST, or EXCEPT.

Questions 1 - 14. Read the following passage carefully before
you choose your answers.

        Above green-flashing plunges of the weir,* and shaken
by the thunder below, lilies, golden and white, were swaying
at anchor among the reeds. Meadowsweet** hung from the
banks thick with weed and training bramble, and there also
hung a daughter of Earth. Her face was shaded by a broad
straw-hat with a flexible brim that left her lips and chin in the
sun, and sometimes nodding, sent forth a light of promising
eyes. Across her shoulders, and behind, flowed large loose
curls, brown in shadow, almost golden where the ray touched
them. She was simply dressed, befitting decency and the season. On a closer inspection you might see that her lips were
stained. This blooming young person was regaling on dewberries.*** They grew between the bank and the water. Apparently she found the fruit abundant, for her hand was making pretty progress to her mouth. Fastidious youth, which
shudders and revolts at woman plumping her exquisite pro-
portions on bread-and-butter, and would (we must suppose)
joyfully have her quite scraggy to have her quite poetical, can
hardly object to dewberries. Indeed the act of eating them is
dainty and induces musing. The dewberry is a sister to the
lotus**** and an innocent sister. You eat; mouth, eye, and
hand are occupied, and the undrugged mind free to roam. And
so it was with the damsel who knelt there. The little skylark

went up above her, all song, to the smooth southern cloud lying along the blue; from a dewy copse standing dark over her nodding hat, the blackbird fluted, calling to her with thrice mellow note; the kingfisher flashed emerald out of green osiers;***** a bow-winged heron traveled aloft, searching solitude; a boat slipped towards her, containing a dreamy youth, and still she plucked the fruit, and ate, and mused, as if no fairy prince were invading her territories, and as if she wished not for one, or knew not her wishes. Surrounded by the green shaven meadows, the pastoral summer buzz, the weir-fall's thundering white, amid the breath and beauty of wildflowers, she was a bit of lovely human life in a fair setting — a terrible attraction. The Magnetic Youth leaned round to note his proximity to the weir-piles, and beheld the sweet vision. Stiller and stiller grew Nature, as at the meeting of two electric clouds. Her posture was so graceful that, though he was making straight for the weir, he dared not dip a scull. Just then one most enticing dewberry caught her eye. He was floating by unheeded, and saw that her hand stretched low and could not gather what it sought. A stroke from his right brought him beside her. The damsel glanced up dismayed, and her whole shape trembled over the brink. Richard sprang from his boat into the water. Pressing a hand beneath her foot, which she had thrust against the crumbling wet sides of the bank to save herself, he enabled her to recover her balance, and gain safe earth, wither, emboldened by the incident, touching her finger tips, he followed her.

*weir: dam ** meadowsweet: a plant of the rose family
***dewberries: blackberries
****lotos: lotus, the fruit of which was said to induce drowsiness and forgetfulness
*****osiers: willows

1. In the very beginning of the passage, the author's purpose is to
   (A) create a metaphor for the girl and her actions
   (B) foreshadow the meeting between the two youth
   (C) attract attention to the various flowers on the river
   (D) create a complete picture of the surroundings
   (E) give commentary of the actions of the two youth

2. In the opening lines of the passage, the author illustrates how Nature has a sympathetic relationship with

> (A) "the green-flashing plunges of the weir"
> (B) "The Magnetic Youth"
> (C) "meadowsweet"
> (D) "a daughter of the Earth"
> (E) a "regaling on dewberries"

3. In the first half of the passage, the speaker's description of the "daughter of the Earth" includes

> (A) personality descriptions
> (B) explanations of her family line
> (C) assertions about her life
> (D) spiritual characteristics representing her relationship with the youth
> (E) physical characteristics representing her relationship with Nature

4. In the context of line "from a dewy copse standing dark over her nodding hat, the blackbird fluted, calling to her with thrice mellow note" the author chose to have a "copse" in the setting because he wanted to

> (A) describe a thicket of brush
> (B) make a dark background that would increase the appeal of the magnetic youth
> (C) picture the flowing trees in the brush
> (D) provide a background that would enhance the beauty of the young woman
> (E) create a setting that would overpower the woman

5. All of the following descriptions describe the young woman as "a bit of lovely human life in a fair setting" EXCEPT:

> (A) "a dreamy youth"
> (B) "a light of promising eyes"
> (C) "a magnificent youth"
> (D) "exquisite proportions"
> (E) flowed large loose curls"

6. Which of the following is the antecedent of "they" in the line "They grew between the bank and the water" ?

> (A) lotos
> (B) meadowsweets
> (C) dewberries
> (D) fruit
> (E) daisies

7. Toward the end of the poem, the phrase "brought him beside her" can best be interpreted as" a reference to the speaker's

(A) regret that they were no longer alone
(B) awareness of their personal attraction
(C) skepticism about wanting to make a turn in his boat
(D) anticipation of their unity
(E) view of their contrasted meaning

8. The use of the phrase "fastidious youth . . . can hardly object to dewberries" has the effect of

(A) making a connection between attractiveness and eating
(B) clarifying the meaning of "fastidious"
(C) repeating the earlier references to "dewberries"
(D) exposing the speaker's opinions on youth
(E) revealing the speaker's attitude toward "dewberries"

9. All of the following show how the young girl is one with the Earth EXCEPT:

(A) "the blackbird fluted, calling to her with thrice mellow note;"
(B) "the kingfisher flashed emerald out of green osiers;"
(C) "a bow-winged heron traveled aloft, searching solitude;"
(D) "a boat slipped towards her, containing a dreamy youth"
(E) "she plucked the fruit, and ate, and mused"

10. The sentence beginning "The Magnetic Youth . . . ." serves primarily to

(A) get the attention of the reader
(B) convince the reader that
(C) distinguish the two characters in the passage
(D) actively describe a character
(E) specify how

11. The contrast between the young woman and the young man is emphasized by the young man's

(A) sense of humor and the woman's innocence
(B) self confidence and the woman's lack of self knowledge
(C) appreciation and the woman's lack of comprehension
(D) admiration and the woman's beauty
(E) madness and the woman's lack of wit

12. All of the following descriptions show that the two were meant for each other EXCEPT

    (A) "brought him beside her"

    (B) "the meeting of two electric clouds"

    (C) "a pressing hand beneath her foot"

    (D) "smooth southern cloud lying along the blue"

    (E) "a bit of lovely human life"

13. The narrator's perspective in the passage is that of

    (A) an acquaintance of the girl

    (B) an uninvolved storyteller

    (C) an appreciative eyewitness

    (D) a commentator on the teens' actions

    (E) an acquaintance of the boy

14. What is the significance of the author's allusion to "lotos"?

    (A) Lotos is a fruit common to the dewberry.

    (B) Lotos is a fruit different than the dewberry.

    (C) Lotos, a fruit mentioned in The Odyssey, when eaten, causes drowsiness and forgetfulness

    (D) Lotos is a fruit that kept the men alive on the long voyage of The Odyssey.

    (E) Lotos is a fruit eaten by the sirens in The Odyssey.

Questions 15-25: Carefully read the following two versions of the poem written by D. H. Lawrence before choosing your answers:

(1) "Piano"

Somewhere beneath that piano's superb sleek black

Must hide my mother's piano, little and brown, with the back

That stood close to the wall, and the front's faded silk both torn,

And the keys with little hollows, that my mother's fingers had worn.

(5)   Softly, in the shadows, a woman is singing to me

Quietly, through the years I have crept back to see

A child sitting under the piano, in the boom of the shaking strings

Pressing the little poised feet of the mother who smiles as she sings.

The full-throated woman has chosen a winning, living song

(10)   And surely the heart that is in me must belong
        To the old Sunday evenings, when darkness wan-
                dered outside
        And hymns gleamed on our warm lips, as we watched
                mother's fingers glide . . .

        Or this is my sister at home in the old front room
        Singing love's first surprised gladness, alone in the
                gloom.
(15)   She will start when she sees me, and blushing, spread
                out her hands
        To cover my mouth's raillery, till I'm bound in her
                shame's heartspun bands.

        A woman is singing me a wild Hungarian air
        And her arms, and her bosom, and the whole of her
                soul is bare,
        And the great black piano is clamouring as my
                mother's could never clamour.

(2) Piano

        Softly, in the dusk, a woman is singing to me;
        Taking me back down the vista of years, till I see
        A child sitting under the piano, in the boom of the
                tingling strings
        And pressing the small, poised feet of a mother who
                smiles as she sings.

(5)   In spite of myself, the insidious mastery of song
        Betrays me back, till the heart of me weeps to belong
        To the old Sunday evenings at home, with winter out-
                side
        And hymns in the cozy parlour, the tinkling piano
                our guide.

        So now it is vain for the singer to burst into clamour
(10)   With the great black piano appassionato. The glam-
                our
        Of childish days is upon me, my manhood is cast
        Down in the flood of remembrance, I weep like a child
                for the past.

15. The speaker's primary purpose in the first stanza of the first poem is to:

    (A) describe a series of emotions that the piano sparked in him from his detested childhood

    (B) portray the fond remembrance which led him to yearn for his lost childhood peace

    (C) depict his mother's love for music and the piano and how she passed it on to him

    (D) comment on the unhealthy poverty of his childhood which he paradoxically misses

    (E) give character to his new piano and to severely criticize a piano of old

16. All of the following phrases illustrate what the poet meant by "piano" EXCEPT:

    (A) "little and brown"

    (B) superb sleek black" (D) "wild Hungarian"

    (C) "great black"   (E) "boom of the tingling strings"

17. All of the following are synonyms for the feelings associated with the word "impassionato" EXCEPT:

    (A) agitated

    (B) commenced   (D) commoved

    (C) stirred   (E) fired

18. Which of the following best describes the tone of the speaker's voice in stanza two of the second poem when he says "In spite of myself, the insidious mastery of song betrays me back"?

    (A) remorseful due to remembering

    (B) disappointed due to intelligence

    (C) sympathetic bordering on pity

    (D) remorseful from happy memories

    (E) indifference based on recollections

19. The speaker in the second poem can be described a person who

    (A) is constantly remembering the past

    (B) is actually more interested in his mother's piano than his own

    (C) has talent both as a pianist and a writer

    (D) is motivated very differently from his sister

    (E) aspires to greatness but knows he will never achieve it

20. The goal of the poet was to make the second poem better than the first. An example of how he did this can be seen in the way he does which of the following to the second poem?

    (A) adds more rhetorical and stylistic strategies
    (B) expresses his longing for the past more
    (C) refers to the present more
    (D) conveys a brighter, more meaningful message
    (E) uses more imagery, making it brighter

21. The style of the line "So now it is vain for the singer to burst into clamour" (line 9), Piano (2) can best described as

    (A) technical and abstruse
    (B) learned and educated
    (C) colloquial and conversational
    (D) pedestrian and imaginative
    (E) lofty and imposing

22. In the last stanza of the second poem, the speaker seems to want to

    (A) convince the reader of the speaker's guilt and loss
    (B) stimulate the reader's attention through the use of specific detail
    (C) use abstract reasoning to convince the reader of the speaker's authority
    (D) illustrate the events of one individual's life to insinuate something about other lives
    (E) conclude the poem in a manner that leaves the reader in suspense

23. The speaker's primary purpose in the last stanza of each poem is to

    (A) portray an unbelievable event
    (B) relate the importance of intelligence
    (C) characterize an idyllic era
    (D) enhance the mastery of memory
    (E) illuminate the melancholy of remembrance

24. The style of both poems can be best described as

    (A) subjective historical commentaries
    (B) melodramatic episodes
    (C) allegorical fables
    (D) a massing of factual information
    (E) extended examples of blended families

25. The poet uses "clamour" in the last stanza of the second poem as a symbol for
    (A) his presented detested life
    (B) his present complicated life
    (C) his present glamorous life
    (D) his love of music
    (E) his advice to aspiring pianists

26. In the last stanza of the second poem, a primary rhetorical strategy of the speaker is to
    (A) convince the reader of the speaker's feelings of guilt and loss
    (B) stimulate the reader's attention through the use of precise details
    (C) use abstract reasoning to convince the reader of the speaker's authority
    (D) conclude the poem in a fulfilling manner
    (E) use logical appeals to teach a lesson

Questions 27-37: Carefully read the following poem by Adrienne Rich before choosing your answers:

"Storm Warnings"

The glass has been falling all afternoon,
And knowing better than the instrument
What winds are walking overhead, what zone
Of gray unrest is moving across the land,
(5) I leave the book upon a pillowed chair
And walked from window to closed window, watch-
ing
Boughs strain against the sky

And think again, as often when the air
Moves inward toward a silent core of waiting,
(10) How with a single purpose time has traveled
By secret currents of the undiscerned
Into this polar realm. Weather abroad
And weather in the heart alike come on
Regardless of prediction.

(15) Between foreseeing and averting change
Lies all the mastery of elements
Which clocks and weatherglasses cannot alter.
Time in hand is not control of time,

Nor shattered fragments of an instrument
(20)   A proof against the wind; the wind will rise,
We can only close the shutters.

I draw the curtains as the sky goes black
And set a match to candles sheathed in glass
Against the keyhole draught, the insistent whine
(25)   Of weather through the unsealed aperture.
This is our sole defense against the season;
These are the things that we have learned to do
Who lived in troubled regions.

27. The main focus of the poem is
    (A) description of the literal and figurative meanings
        of "the storm"
    (B) characterization of our sole defense against the
        season
    (C) portrayal of the storm moving across the land
    (D) commentary on the insistent whine of the weather
    (E) portray of the positive effects of storms

28. Lines 1-6 have which of the following effects?
    (A) It provides knowledge of how weather devices
        work.
    (B) It grabs the reader's attention, encouraging inter-
        est in the poem.
    (C) It emphasizes that the poem is about weather.
    (D) It has no other effect other than to serve as an
        introduction for the poem.
    (E) It sets a derogatory tone for the rest of the poem.

29. What is the meaning of "Weather abroad/And weather in
the heart alike come on/Regardless of prediction" (.lines 12-
14)?
    (A) The weather outside can be predicted.
    (B) Neither the weather outside nor the emotions in-
        side can be predicted by anyone.
    (C) Weather abroad doesn't affect the weather near
        us.
    (D) Only the Polar Realm can affect the weather.
    (E) Regardless of what we predict, there will never be
        storms.

30. In the second stanza, the "Polar Realm" refers to
    (A) the North Pole
    (B) your heart
    (C) the storm
    (D) the people around you
    (E) northern Minnesota

31. Which of the following is true about winds in the third stanza?
    (A) Personification is used to enhance the meaning.
    (B) Descriptions of the wind create an illusion of fear.
    (C) Illustrations are based on visual qualities only.
    (D) Images are more positive than negative.
    (E) Adjectives describe spiritual rather than physical aspects.

32. The sentence beginning with "This is our sole defense" serves primarily to
    (A) indicate the poet's negative attitude toward the bitterness of the storms
    (B) display how the heart is our strongest defense against society's unpredictable coldness
    (C) distinguish the "sole defense" of the heart and the house
    (D) convince the audience that storm warnings serve a specific purpose as a helpful precaution
    (E) reflect the unsealed aperture as described by the poet

33. Which of the following is the grammatical antecedent of "this" (line 26)?
    (A) candles sheathed in glass
    (B) instruments rising and falling
    (C) curtains drawn for protection
    (D) shutters on the windows
    (E) clocks and weatherglasses

34. The last three lines of the poem (lines 26 - 28) serve what purpose?
    (A) to leave an opening for another stanza
    (B) to tell how to defend against the weather
    (C) to end the poem with a line that explains the meaning of the poem
    (D) to explain that people who live in troubled regions are the only ones that can deal with the weather
    (E) to state that there is only one way to deal with weather and it has to be learned

35. Although this poem is about protection against the physical aspects of the harsh weather, it is also about

    (A) the storm of cruelty thrown upon our hearts by those around us

    (B) the need to protect our home and our possessions

    (C) the different ways we can avoid an emotional storm

    (D) the boughs of our heart fluttering in the breeze

    (E) the vast storm of emotions circulating within our hears

36. All the following are examples of the descriptive and parallel style of the passage EXCEPT:

    (A) "what winds are walking overhead"

    (B) "gray unrest is moving across the land"

    (C) " I draw the curtains as the sky goes black"

    (D) "By secret curtains of the undiscerned"

    (E) "regardless of prediction"

37. The speaker of the poem can best be described as a person who

    (A) is committed to "the things we have learned to do"

    (B) has feelings of both remorse and regret

    (C) is committed to describing the literal and metaphorical aspects of storm warnings

    (D) wants people to know how dangerous and merciless storms can be

    (E) illustrates a positive picture of storms

38. The primary purpose of the passage is to

    (A) warn readers of an oncoming storm

    (B) encourage readers to pay no heed to the storm warnings

    (C) parallel the emotional and physical aspects of storm warnings

    (D) show that clocks and weatherglasses cannot alter storms

    (E) convince people that the millennium will result in troubled times

<u>Questions 39-50:</u>   Carefully read the following opening of a novel before choosing your answers:

Dombey sat in the corner of the darkened room in the great armchair by the bedside, and Son lay tucked up warm in a little basket bedstead, carefully disposed on a low settee immediately in front of the fire and close to it, as if his constitution were analogous to that of a muffin, and it was essential to toast him brown while he was very new.

Dombey was about eight and forty years of age. Son about eight and forty minutes. Dombey was rather bald, rather red, and though a handsome well-made man, too stern and pompous in appearance to be prepossessing. Son was very bald, and very red, and though (of course) an undeniably fine infant, somewhat crushed and spotty in his general effect, as yet. On the brow of Dombey, Time and his brother Care had set some marks, as on a tree that was to come down in good time — remorseless twins they are for striding through their human forests, notching as they go — while the Countenance of Son was crossed and recrossed with a thousand little creases, which the same deceitful Time would take delight in smoothing out and wearing away with the flat part of his scythe, as a preparation of the surface for his deeper operations.

Dombey, exulting in the long-looked-for event, jingled and jingled the heavy gold watch-chain that depended from below his trim blue coat, whereof the buttons sparkled phosphorescently in the feeble rays of the distant fire. Son, with his little fists curled up and clenched, seemed, in his feeble way, to be squaring at existence for having come upon him so unexpectedly.

"The house will once again, Mrs. Dombey," said Mr. Dombey, "be not only in name but in fact Dombey and Son; Dombey and Son!"

The words had such a softening influence that he appended a term of endearment to Mrs. Dombey's name (though not without some hesitation, as being a man but little used to that form of address) and said, "Mrs. Dombey, my — my dear."

A transient flush of faint surprise overspread the sick lady's face as she raised her eyes towards him.

"He will be christened Paul, my — Mrs. Dombey — of course.

She feebly echoed, "Of course," or rather expressed it by the motion of her lips, and closed her eyes again.

"His father's name, Mrs. Dombey, and his grandfather's! I wish his grandfather were alive this day!" And again he said "Dombey and Son," in exactly the same tone as before.

Those three words conveyed the one idea of Mr. Dombey's life. The earth was made for Dombey and Son to trade in, and the son and moon were made to give them light. Rivers and seas were formed to float their ships; rainbows gave them promise of fair weather; winds blew for or against their enterprises; stars and planets circled in the orbits to pre-serve inviolate a system of which they were the centre. Common abbreviations took new meanings in his eyes, and had sole reference to them: A. D. had no concern with anno Domini, but stood for anno Dombei — and Son.

39. In the phrase "as if his constitution were analogous to that of a muffin" (paragraph one), the word "constitution" refers to the son's

    (A) disposition

    (B) station in life   (D) physical state

    (C) actual location   (E) mental awareness

40. When the narrator uses the phrase "Son was. . . (of course) an undeniably fine infant" (paragraph two), he is trying to

    (A) ridicule the belief that all infants are perfect

    (B) tell the reader what kind of son Dombey had

    (C) compliment Dombey on such a fine child

    (D) tell the reader to try to fit into the situation

    (E) compare the son to his father Dombey

41. In the second paragraph, all of the following are examples of parallel images created by the author of Dombey and Son EXCEPT: (A) "Dombey was about eight and forty years of age. Son about eight and forty minutes.

    (B) "Dombey was rather bald, rather red . . . . Son was very bald, and very red"

    (C) "on the brow of Dombey, Time and his brother Care had set some marks . . . while the Countenance of Son was crossed and recrossed with a thousand little creases"

    (D) "remorseless twins they are for striding through their human forests, notching as they go"

    (E) "the same deceitful Time would take delight in smoothing out and wearing away with the flat part of his scythe, as a preparation of the surface for his deeper operations"

42. In the second paragraph, the author creates images so that the reader can
>   (A) visualize the characters
>   (B) improve themselves after reading
>   (C) hear stories about them
>   (D) try to fit into the situation
>   (E) get an early exposure to the story

43. The phrase "A transient flush of faint surprise " makes use of which stylistic device?
>   (A) alliteration
>   (B) simile
>   (C) metaphor
>   (D) allusion
>   (E) imagery

44. The use of the phrase "long-looked-for event" has the effect of
>   (A) clarifying the deep anticipation a childless couple had for the birth of their first child
>   (B) characterizing the speaker as an impatient man
>   (C) forcing the reader to infer that Dombey would be a dead-beat dad
>   (D) repeating earlier references to Dombey's happy childhood
>   (E) exposing Dombey's uncertainty about parenting

45. In the last paragraph, the phrase "the earth was made for Dombey and Son" can best be interpreted as a reference to the narrator's
>   (A) regret that Dombey had to wait so many years for a son
>   (B) awareness of Dombey's happiness
>   (C) skepticism about the true source of Dombey's happiness
>   (D) opinion that Dombey and Son would be successful in life
>   (E) happiness over the birth of Dombey's son.

46. By using the phrase "A. D. had no concern with anno Domini, but stood for anno Dombei — and Son," the speaker draws attention to the fact that

    (A) Dombey thinks he is more important than time itself

    (B) Dombey puts too much importance on the birth on his son

    (C) Dombey thought his name was better in Latin

    (D) Dombey's son was born after Christ

    (E) Dombey thought that time was unimportant now that Son was born

47. In the last paragraph. a primary rhetorical strategy of the author is to

    (A) use hyperbole to draw attention to his view of Dombey

    (B) use imagery to reveal Dombey's thoughts

    (C) convey Dombey's view of the world through Dombey's thoughts

    (D) use Dombey's desires to portray his character

    (E) convince the reader that what Dombey thinks is likely to come true

48. Dombey is a character who can be best be described as being

    (A) committed to selfish goals

    (B) more interested in death than life

    (C) talented as both a father and a husband

    (D) committed to being a great father

    (E) focused on achieving greatness

49. The tone that the author creates reflects the author's views that the traditional importance placed on first born sons is all of the following EXCEPT:

    (A) outdated

    (B) ludicrous

    (C) well-founded

    (D) misguided

    (E) quaint

50. All of the following phrases indicate that Dombey's world was centered around himself EXCEPT:

    (A) "the earth was made for Dombey and Son"

    (B) " the son and moon were made to give them light"

    (C) "Rivers and seas were formed to float their ships"

    (D) 'rainbows gave them promise of fair weather'

    (E) he "had no concern with anno Domini"

Practice Test 1:
"Use A PEN"

ENGLISH
LITERATURE AND COMPOSITION
SECTION II
Time — 2 hours
Number of questions — 3
Percent of total grade — 55

Each question counts as one-third of the total essay score.
Question 1 Essay — Suggested time. . . . . 40 minutes
Question 2 Essay — Suggested time. . . . . 40 minutes
Question 3 Essay — Suggested time. . . . . 40 minutes

ENGLISH LITERATURE AND COMPOSITION
SECTION II
Total Time — 2 hours
Question I
(Suggested time — 40 minutes. This question
counts one-third of the total)

Read the following famous soliloquy from
Shakespeare's play *Hamlet,* Act 3, scene 1, and its parody from
The Adventures of Huckleberry Finn that follows. Then write a
carefully organized essay analyzing how similar
Shakespearean phrases (diction) are manipulated by each
writer's different use of syntax to affect meaning and purpose.

Hamlet

> To be, or not to be, that is the question:
> Whether 'tis nobler in the mind to suffer
> The slings and arrows of outrageous fortune,
> Or to take arms against a sea of troubles

(5)
> And by opposing end them. To die, to sleep —
> No more — and by a sleep to say we end
> The heartache and the thousand natural shocks
> That flesh is heir to. 'Tis a consumation
> Devoutly to be wished. To die, to sleep;

(10)
> To sleep, perchance to dream. Ay, there's the rub,
> For in that sleep of death what dreams may come,
> When we have shuffled off this mortal coil,
> Must give us pause. There's the respect
> That makes calamity of so long life.

(15)   For who would bear the whips and scorns of time,
         Th' oppressor's wrong, the proud man's contumely,
         The pangs of disprized love, the law's delay,
         The insolence of office, and the spurns
         That patient merit of th' unworthy takes,
(20)   When he himself might his quietus make
         With a bare bodkin? Who would fardels bear,
         To grunt and swear under a weary life,
         But that the dread of something after death,
         The undiscovered country from whose bourn
(25)   No traveler returns, puzzles the will,
         And makes it rather bear those ills we have
         Than fly to others that we know not of?
         Thus conscience does make cowards of us all;
         And thus the native hue of resolution
(30)   Is sickled o'er with the pale cast of thought,
         And enterprises of great pitch and moment
         With this regard their currents turn awry
         And lose the name of action. — Soft you now,
         The fair Ophelia, Nymph, in thy orisons
(35)   Be all my sins remembered.

3 slings (missiles) **10 rub** (Literally, an obstacle in the game of bowls) **12 shuffled** (sloughed, cast) **12 coil** (turmoil) **13 respect** (consideration) **14 of so long life** (so long-lived, also suggesting that long life itself is a calamity) **15 time** (the world we live in) **16 contumely** (insolent abuse) **17 disprized** (unvalued) **18 office** (officialdom) **18 spurns** insults) **19 of th' unworthy takes** (receives from unworthy persons) **20 quietus** (death) **21 a bare** merely a) **21 bodkin** (dagger) **21 fardels** (burden) **24 bourn** (boundary) **29 native hue** (natural color **30 cast** (tinge, shade of color) **31 pitch** (height - as of a falcon's flight) **31 moment** (importance) **32 regard** (respect, consideration) **32 currents** (courses) **33 Soft you** (i.e. Wait a minute, gently) **34 orisons** (prayers)

from *The Adventures of Huckleberry Finn*
Duke:

        To be, or not to be; that is the bare bodkin
        That makes calamity of so long life;
        For who would fardels bear, till Birnam Wood do come
            to Dunsinane,
        But that the fear of something after death
(5)   Murders the innocent sleep,
        Great nature's second course,
        And makes us rather sling the arrows of outrageous
            fortune
        Than fly to others that we know not of.
        There's the respect must give us pause:
(10)   Wake Duncan with thy knocking! I would thou
            couldst;
        For who would bear the whips and scorns of time,
        The oppressor's wrong, the proud man's contumely,
        The law's delay, and the quietus which his pangs might
            take,
        In the dead waste and middle of the night, when
            churchyards yawn
(15)   In customary suits of solemn black,
        But that the undiscovered country from whose bourn
            no traveler returns,
        Breathes forth contagion on the world,
        And thus the native hue of resolution, like the poor
            cat i' the adage,
        Is sickled o'er with care,
(20)   And all the clouds that lowered o'er our housetops,
        With his regard their currents turn awry,
        And lose the name of action.
        'Tis a consummation devoutly to be wished. But soft
            you, fair Ophelia:
        Ope not thy ponderous and marble jaws,
(25)   But get thee to a nunnery — go!

Question II
(Suggested time — 40 minutes. This question
counts one-third of the total)

Since the publication of "The Custom House" created such a negative community reaction, Hawthorne made this statement as a preface to his Second edition: "As the public disapprobation would weigh very heavily upon him, were he conscious of deserving it, the author begs leave to say that he has carefully read over the introductory pages, with a purpose to alter or expunge whatever might be found amiss, and to make the best reparation in his power for the atrocities of which he has been adjudged guilty. But it appears to him, that the only remarkable features of the sketch are its frank and genuine good humor, and the general accuracy with which he has conveyed his sincere impressions of the characters herein described." And so Hawthorne ends by saying that he has decided to "republish his introductory sketch without the change of a word."

Read the following excerpt from "The Custom House" with the above controversy in mind. Then write a well-organized essay in which you analyze how the author's use of frank humor, selection of details and other resources of language distinguish his negative toward the community and its members described.

As respects the majority of my corps of veterans, there will be no wrong done, if I characterize them generally as a set of wearisome old souls, who had gathered nothing worth preservation from their varied experience of life. They seemed to have flung away all the golden grain of practical wisdom, which they had enjoyed so many opportunities of harvesting, and most carefully to have stored their memories with the husks. They spoke with far more interest and unction of their morning's breakfast, or yesterday's, today's or tomorrow's dinner, than of the shipwreck of forty or fifty years ago, and all the world's wonders which they had witnessed with their youthful eyes.

The father of the custom house . . . was a certain permanent inspector. He was a man of fourscore years, or thereabouts, and certainly one of the most wonderful specimens of wintergreen that you would be likely to discover in a lifetime's

search. With his florid cheek, his compact figure, smartly ar-
rayed in a bright-buttoned blue coat, his brisk and vigorous
step, and his hale and hearty aspect, altogether he seemed —
not young, indeed — but a kind of new contrivance of Mother
Nature in the shape of a man, whom age and infirmity had no
business to touch. His voice and laugh, which perpetually re-
echoed through the Custom House, had nothing of the tremu-
lous quaver and cackle of an old man's utterance; they came
strutting out of his lungs, like the crow of a cock, or the blast of
a clarion. Looking at him merely as an animal, — and there
was very little else to look at, — he was a most satisfactory
object, from the thorough healthfulness and wholesomeness
of his system, and his capacity, at that extreme age, to enjoy
all, or nearly all, the delights which he had ever aimed at, or
conceived of. The careless security of his life at the Custom
House, on a regular income, and with but slight and infrequent
apprehensions of removal, had no doubt contributed to make
time pass lightly over him. The original and more potent
causes, however, lay in the rare perfection of his animal nature, the moderate proportion of intellect, and the very trifling
admixture of moral and spiritual ingredients; these latter qualities, indeed, being in barely enough measure to keep the old
gentleman from walking on all-fours. . . .

He was, in truth, a rare phenomenon; so perfect, in
one point of view; so shallow, so delusive, so impalpable, such
an absolute nonentity, in every other. My conclusion was that
he had no soul, no heart, no mind; nothing . . . but instincts.

It is time to quit this sketch; on which, however, I
should be glad to dwell at considerably more length, because
of all men whom I had ever known, this individual was the
fittest to be a Custom House officer. Most persons, owing to
causes which I may have space to hint at, suffer moral detri-
ment from this peculiar mode of life. The old Inspector was
incapable of it, and, were he to continue in office ti the end of
time, would be just as good as he was then, and sit down to
dinner with just as good an appetite.

Question 3
(Suggested time — 40 minutes. This questions counts
one-third of the total essay score.)

Good writers use symbols because their evocation of
multiple meanings allow the writer to say more with less. Select a novel, play, or long poem in which settings, characters,
actions, objects, motifs, or names suggest something beyond
its literal meaning. Analyze how the author establishes these
as symbols through the use of such clues as repetition, position, or more than routine emphasis. Then explain how the
symbolic meanings fit comfortably into the context of the story.

Choose a novel, play, or long poem by one of the following authors or another author of comparable merit.

Herman Melville	Margaret Atwood
Fydor Dostoevsky	Jane Austen
Arthur Miller	T. S. Eliot
Henry Fielding	Zora Neal Hurston
Henrik Ibsen	Eudora Welty
Tennessee Williams	Anton Chekov
Charles Dickens	Edith Wharton
William Shakespeare	Edgar Allen Poe
Joseph Conrad	Robert Frost
William Faulkner	Sylvia Plath
Ernest Hemingway	Willa Cather
George Orwell	Sandra Cisneros
John Bunyan	Toni Morrison
Maxine Hong Kingston	Alice Walker
Nathaniel Hawthorne	Virginia Woolf
Albert Camus	Richard Wright

Answers and Explanations

To Practice Test 1:
Section II: Essay

Checklist for
Question 1

from Hamlet's Soliloquy (William Shakespeare) and
the Duke's parody of the same soliloquy (Mark Twain)

STEP 1:   Check each item listed below which accurately describes the positive aspects of the essay being graded. Add one point for each item checked from the list. This side describes the basic requirements for a well-written essay. (Grader one should check column one. Grader two should check column two):

___-___1. The writer demonstrates a perceptive understanding of the meaning and purpose for each soliloquy.

___-___2. The writer analyzes how diction and syntax affect meaning and purpose in each soliloquy.

___-___3. The writer demonstrates a perceptive understanding of how similar diction is manipulated by each writer's different use of syntax to affect meaning and purpose.

___-___4. The writer makes apt (a minimum of three embedded bits of quotes per paragraph) and specific (detailed and appropriate) reference to the texts.

___-___5. The writer offers a convincing interpretation of the purpose for each soliloquy.

___-___6. The writer demonstrates an ability to read perceptively by saying something beyond the easy and obvious to grasp

___-___7. The writer demonstrates a control over the virtues of effective communication, including the language unique to literary criticism.

___-___8. The writer's organization is implicit and original, yet communicates a clear message.

___-___9. The writer's diction, sentence structure, and grammar aid in communicating a clear message.

MAXIMUM SCORE RESULTS: Grader 1 _____
MAXIMUM SCORE RESULTS: Grader 2 _____

STEP 1:   Check each item listed below which accurately describes the positive aspects of the essay being graded. Add one point for each item checked from the list. This side describes the basic requirements for a well-written essay. (Grader one should check column one. Grader two should check column two):

___-___1. The writer's definition of meaning is oversimplified or vague or omits any discussion of the differing purposes for each soliloquy.

___-___2. The writer discusses the use of diction and syntax with limited purpose or with inappropriate examples.

___-___3. The connection between language and meaning is less clear than those of the top-scoring essays.

___-___4. The writer's use of quotes is awkward, inappropriate, or uninteresting.

___-___5. The writer misreads the meaning or purpose of one or both of the soliloquies.

___-___6. The writer's interpretation is not as persuasive as those of the highest-scoring essays.

___-___7. The writer misuses the literary term(s) addressed in the question or omits them partially or entirely.

___-___8. The organization of this essay is less original or implicit than those of the top-scoring essays.

___-___9. The essay reveals consistent weakness in grammar and/or other basic elements of composition.

RESULTS:

Grader 1: _____ - _____ = _____
                Step 1 Score   Step 2 Score
Grader 2: _____ - _____ = _____
                Step 1 Score   Step 2 Score

Grader 1 Score + Grader 2 Score = _____

Above sum /
divided by 2 =

Score for essay

Answers and Explanations

To Practice Test 1: Section II: AP Rubrics

Rubrics for Question 1

from Hamlet's Soliloquy (William Shakespeare) and the Duke's parody of the same soliloquy (Mark Twain

8-9   The students who wrote these essays demonstrate a clear understanding of how Shakespearean diction is manipulated differently by each of the authors to achieve their purpose. The writer presents a clear and relevant thesis — correctly identifying the meaning (or lack of meaning) of each soliloquy — supported by apt and specific evidence from the texts. The organization of these high-scoring essays is implicit and clear. Thoroughly convincing, this prose demonstrates the writer's ability to control a wide range of the elements of effective writing, but need not be without flaws.

6-7   These essays also correctly identify the contrasting purposes of each soliloquy and analyze how the different uses of syntax affect their respective meanings, but the thesis is less specific than the top-scoring essay. Typically they analyze fewer Shakespearean phrases, making the evidence less convincing. The importance of syntax in creating meaning may also be less clear than the top-scoring essay. The organization is less implicit than those of the highest-scoring essays. A few lapses in diction, syntax, or use of literary language may be present, but usually the prose of essays scoring a 6 conveys their writer's ideas clearly.

5   These essays are superficial. They define the meaning of the soliloquies in a typically pedestrian fashion. They deal with the assigned tasks of the question, but they have little to say beyond the easy and obvious to grasp. Their understanding of the importance of syntax in creating meaning may be vague, mechanical, or inadequately supported. While the writing is sufficient to convey the writer's thoughts, these essays are not as well-conceived, organized, or developed as the upper half papers. Often they reveal simplistic thinking and/or immature writing.

3-4   These lower-half essays may not answer the entire question. Frequently they misrepresent the purpose of one or both of the soliloquies, analyze syntax and diction with limited purpose or accuracy, or catalogue various phrases in the soliloquies without relating them to purpose and meaning. The prose of essays scoring a 4 usually conveys their writers' ideas adequately, but may demonstrate uncertain control over the qualities of college-level composition. They usually contain recurrent stylistic flaws and lack persuasive evidence from the texts.

1-2   These essays demonstrate little or no success in portraying meaning and purpose and in analyzing how they are conveyed. Some substitute a simpler task, such as paraphrasing the passage or diction and syntax in general. In addition, they are poorly written on several counts and may contain distracting errors in grammar and mechanics. Frequently, they are unacceptably brief. While some attempt may have been made to answer the question, the writer's observations are presented with little clarity, organization, or supporting evidence. Essays that are especially inexact, vacuous, ill-organized, illogically organized and/or mechanically unsound should receive a score of 1.

Answers and Explanations

To Practice Test 1:
Section II: Results
of Essay 1

from *Hamlet's* Soliloquy (William Shakespeare) and the Duke's parody of the same soliloquy (Mark Twain)

Following are examples of how the writer could demonstrate a perceptive understanding of the meaning and purpose of each soliloquy, analyzing how similar diction is manipulated by each writer's different use of syntax to affect meaning and purpose.

    A. Although both soliloquies use the same diction, Shakespeare's is more conventional in purpose, arranging the diction in normal syntax to convey Hamlet's state of mind.

    B. Twain's parody of Hamlet's soliloquy has a more satiric purpose, arranging the diction of Shakespeare in nonsensical syntax to make fun of the character of the Duke.

    C. With a few obvious changes in syntax, Shakespeare's melodious diction becomes meaningless in the Duke's rendition.

Following are examples of how the writer could make apt (a minimum of three embedded bits of quotes per paragraph) and specific (detailed and appropriate) reference to the text, offering a convincing interpretation of the purpose and meaning for each soliloquy.

    A. The conning Duke plods through the parody using such phrases as "I would thou couldst" and "ope not thy ponderous and marble jaws," sounding like Shakespeare to the naive audience but appearing idiotic to the educated reader.

    B. Whereas Hamlet ends poetically by asking through prayers "be all my sins remembered," the Duke ends by quoting a phrase that appears elsewhere in Shakespeare's play, "Get thee to a nunnery -- go!"

Following are examples of how the writer could demonstrate an ability to read perceptively by saying something beyond the easy and obvious to grasp.

A. This comparison reveals that even though words are well-chosen, if they are not arranged in careful order, the result is confusion.

B. The literal meaning of the reordered diction of the Duke's soliloquy creates humor. Literally, in the first line, the Duke is pondering whether to be, or not to be a knife (bodkin)!

C. The placement of the words create important, but drastically different significance to each soliloquy.

Correct the following sentences in which the writer demonstrates a lack of control over the virtues of effective communication, including the language unique to literary criticism, the writer's diction, sentence structure, and grammar:

A. To be a good writer, one must first establish a creditable basis.

B. These two masters of their trade use similar phrases to create tremendously different ideas and these ideas are given to the reader.

C. Even though only Hamlet's soliloquy has meaning, both have purpose, for no one says nothing for no reason.

D. The Duke's version is totally the opposite than Hamlet's.

E. The Duke has a version slightly comparing to Hamlet's.

F. The placement of the words in each soliloquy cause different significance to each one -- Hamlet's words are arranged to tell of his unstable mind; The Duke's words are arranged to tell of his conning character.

Answers and Explanations

To Practice Test 1:
Section II: Essay

Checklist for
Question 2

from Nathaniel Hawthorne's "The Custom House"

STEP 1:   Check each item listed below which accurately describes the positive aspects of the essay being graded. Add one point for each item checked from the list. This side describes the basic requirements for a well-written essay. (Grader one should check column one. Grader two should check column two):

___-___1. The writer demonstrates a perceptive understanding of the complexity of Hawthorne's attitude toward the community and its members.

___-___2. The writer analyzes how frank humor, selection of detail, and other resources of the language distinguish Hawthorne's attitude.

___-___3. The thesis clearly shows the connection between Hawthorne's attitude toward the community and its members and the language devices used to convey that attitude.

___-___4. The writer makes apt (a minimum of three embedded bits of quotes per paragraph) and specific (detailed and appropriate) reference to the text.

___-___5. The writer offers a convincing interpretation of the power of Hawthorne's sketch.

___-___6. The writer demonstrates an ability to read perceptively by saying something beyond the easy and obvious to grasp.

___-___7. The writer demonstrates a control over the virtues of effective communication, including the language unique to literary criticism.

___-___8. The writer's organization is implicit and original, yet communicates a clear message.

___-___9. The writer's diction, sentence structure, and grammar aid in communicating a clear message.

MAXIMUM SCORE RESULTS: Grader 1 _____
MAXIMUM SCORE RESULTS: Grader 2 _____

STEP 2:   Check each item below which accurately describes the negative aspects of the essay being graded. This side describes how the essay may not be as good as the higher-scoring essays. (Grader one should check column one. Grader two should check column two):

___-___1. The writer demonstrates a perceptive understanding of the complexity of Hawthorne's attitude toward the community and its members.

___-___1. The writer's definition of the attitude is oversimplified or vague or omits any discussion of its irony.

___-___2. The writer discusses the rhetorical and stylistic devices with limited purpose or with inappropriate examples.

___-___3. The connection between the evidence and the author's attitude is less clear than those of the top-scoring essays.

___-___4. The writer's use of quotes is awkward, inappropriate, or uninteresting.

___-___5. The writer misreads the meaning of the passage or simply paraphrases the passage with no reference to the language devices used.

___-___6. The writer's interpretation is not as persuasive as those of the highest scoring essays.

___-___7. The writer misuses the literary term(s) addressed in the question or omits them partially or entirely.

___-___8. The organization of this essay is less original or implicit than those of the top-scoring essays.

___-___9. The essay reveals consistent weakness in grammar and/or other basic elements of composition.

RESULTS:

Grader 1: _____ - _____ = _____
          Step 1 Score   Step 2 Score
Grader 2: _____ - _____ = _____
          Step 1 Score   Step 2 Score
Grader 1 Score + Grader 2 Score = _____

Above sum /
divided by 2 =

Score for essay

Answers and Explanations

To Practice Test 1: Section II: AP Rubrics

Rubrics for Question 2

from Nathaniel Hawthorne's "The Custom House"

8-9   The students who wrote these well-organized and well-written essays clearly define Hawthorne's complex attitude toward the community and its members. With apt and specific references to the passage, they will analyze how frank humor, selection of detail, and other resources of the language distinguish Hawthorne's attitude. The organization of these high-scoring essays is implicit and clear. While not without flaws, these papers will demonstrate an understanding of the text and consistent control over the elements of effective composition. These writers read with perception and express their ideas with clarity and skill.

6-7   These papers also correctly define Hawthorne's complex views of the Custom House members, but they are less incisive, developed, or aptly supported than papers in the highest range. Typically they show how some language or rhetorical devices convey that view, but leave out at least one important element, making the evidence less convincing. The connection between the evidence and Hawthorne's attitude may also be less clear than the top-scoring essay. The organization is less implicit than those of the highest scoring essays. A few lapses in diction, syntax, or use of literary language may be present, but usually the prose of these essays conveys their writer's ideas clearly.

5   Customarily, these essays are superficial. They respond to the assigned topics without important errors, but they do not discuss the irony of Hawthorne's passage. The handling of such elements as frank humor, selection of detail, and other resources of the language may be vague, mechanical, or overly generalized. The writing is adequate to convey the writer's thoughts, but these essays are typically pedestrian, not as well-conceived, organized or developed as upper-half papers. Often they reveal simplistic thinking and/or immature writing.

3-4   These lower-half essays may reflect an incomplete understanding of the passage and fail to respond adequately to part or parts of the question. Frequently the discussion of Hawthorne's view is inaccurate or unclear, misguided or undeveloped; these essays may paraphrase rather than analyze. The treatment of frank humor, selection of detail and other resources of the language is likely to be meager and unconvincing. Generally, the writing demonstrates weak control of such elements as diction, organization, syntax, or grammar. These essays typically contain recurrent stylistic flaws and/or misreadings and lack of persuasive evidence from the text.

1-2   These essays compound the weaknesses of the papers in the 3-4 range. These writers seriously misread the passage or fail to respond to the question. Frequently, they are unacceptably brief. Often poorly written on several counts, these essays may contain many distracting errors in grammar and mechanics. Although some attempt may have been made to answer the question, the writer's views typically are presented with little clarity, organization, coherence, or supporting evidence.

Answers and Explanations

To Practice Test 1:
Section II: Results
of Essay 2

from Nathaniel Hawthorne's "The Custom House"

Following are examples of how the writer could demonstrate a perceptive understanding of the complexity of Hawthorne's attitude toward the community and its members, analyzing how the language is used to distinguish this attitude:

A. The author's unintentional humor reveals his negative attitude.

B. The author's admiring words, with their negative connotations, create humor for the objective reader -- horror for the living characters described.

Following are examples of how the writer could make apt (a minimum of three embedded bits of quotes per paragraph) and specific (detailed and appropriate) reference to the text, offering a convincing interpretation of Hawthorne's sketch.

A. The community members "spoke with far more interest and unction" about their daily meals than anything serious, and even seemed to have barely enough moral fiber to keep from "walking on all fours."

B. The "bright-buttoned coat," the "blast of a clarion" in his voice, and the "compact figure" of the representative person contrast the community members' lack of substance.

Following are examples of how the writer could demonstrate an ability to read perceptively by saying something beyond the easy and obvious to grasp.

A. Hawthorne displays a respect for the physical attributes of the community members, but shows an extremely disparaging attitude toward its moral well being.

Do not force the same organization into every essay. Avoid topic sentences that name the device and make a connection to the view, yet say nothing specific. For example:

> A. Selection of detail is used to show Hawthorne's feelings of negativity towards the community.
>
> B. Hawthorne uses frank humor to show his negative attitude.
>
> C. The last language device Hawthorne uses to describe his negative attitude is the use of similes

Rather, the writer's organization should be implicit and original, yet communicating a clear message. The highest scores will discuss the language of the passage in a natural way, attaching an individual interpretation to the writing .

> A. Hawthorne's veterans at the Custom House were men with "varied experience of life" who had lost interest in living.
>
> B. According to Hawthorne, a "moderate proportion of intellect" and a "trifling admixture of moral and spiritual ingredients" were the only attributes that separated "the father of the custom house" from the animals.

Correct the following sentences in which the writer could demonstrate a lack of control over the virtues of effective communication, including the language unique to literary criticism, the writer's diction, sentence structure, and grammar:

> A. Everyone has thoughts about the people around them, but if the thoughts are negative, most people keep them to themselves.
>
> B. In "The Custom House" by Nathaniel Hawthorne, he shows his negative attitude towards the community and its members.
>
> C. Hawthorne's explanation of the man and his community is sort a visual view of how the man looks.
>
> D. He describes the features of the inspector, "his hale and hearty aspect," "whom age and infirmity had no business to touch."
>
> E. The community thought that Hawthorne was comparing the character in such as a way as to make fun of him and the community.

Answers and Explanations

To Practice Test 1:
Section II: Essay

Checklist for
Question 3

Free Response on SYMBOLS

STEP 1:   Check each item listed below which accurately describes the positive aspects of the essay being graded. Add one point for each item checked from the list. This side describes the basic requirements for a well-written essay. (Grader one should check column one. Grader two should check column two):

___-___1. The writer selects a suitable novel or play in which settings, characters, actions, objects, motifs, or names suggest something beyond its literal meaning.

___-___2. The writer presents a reasonable explanation of the meaning of the work.

___-___3. The writer effectively explains how the author establishes these as symbols through the use of such clues as repetition, position, or more than routine emphasis.

___-___4. The writer effectively explains how the symbolic meanings fit comfortably into the context of the story.

___-___5. The writer makes apt and specific reference to the text.

___-___6. The writer avoids plot summary not relevant to the explanation of the role that symbols play in the evocation of multiple meanings in the work.

___-___7. The writer discusses the literary work with sophistication, insight, and understanding.

___-___8. The writer displays consistent control over the language unique to the discussion of symbolism.

___-___9. The writer's diction, sentence structure, organization, and grammar aid in communicating a clear message.

MAXIMUM SCORE RESULTS: Grader 1 _____

MAXIMUM SCORE RESULTS: Grader 2 _____

STEP 2: Check each item below which accurately describes the negative aspects of the essay being graded. This side describes how the essay may not be as good as the higher-scoring essays. (Grader one should check column one. Grader two should check column two):

___-___1. The writer's selection of a symbolically significant play or novel is not as appropriate as those of the higher scoring essays.

___-___2. The writer's explanation of the meaning of the work is less thorough, less specific, or less perceptive than those of the higher scoring essays.

___-___3. The writer's explanation of how the author establishes these as symbols through the use of such clues as repetition, position, or more than routine emphasis may be vague, underdeveloped, or misguided.

___-___4. The writer's explanation of how the symbolic meanings fit comfortably into the context of the story may be less convincing, mechanical, or inadequately related to the work as a whole.

___-___5. The writer's reference to the text lack the specificity of the higher scoring essays.

___-___6. The writer simply paraphrases the meaning of the work with little reference to its symbolic significance.

___-___7. The writer says nothing beyond the easy and obvious to grasp.

___-___8. The writer misuses the literary term(s) necessary to the discussion of symbolism or omits them partially or entirely.

___-___9. The essay contains distracting errors in grammar and mechanics.   RESULTS:

Grader 1: _____ - _____ = _____
                    Step 1 Score   Step 2 Score

Grader 2: _____ - _____ = _____
                    Step 1 Score   Step 2 Score

Grader 1 Score + Grader 2 Score = _____

Above sum /
divided by 2 =

Score for essay

Answers and Explanations

To Practice Test 1:
Section II: AP Rubrics

Rubrics for Question 3

Free Response on SYMBOLISM

8-9   The students who wrote these essays choose appropriate settings, characters, actions, objects, motifs, or names in a novel of play that suggests something beyond its literal meaning. They explain convincingly how these symbols are established by the author to evoke multiple meanings. These papers reflect an understanding of the role of symbolism in fiction and an understanding of the work itself. Superior papers will be specific in their references, cogent in their explications, and free of plot summary not directly relevant to the role that symbolism plays in the work. These essays may not be without flaws, but they demonstrate the writer's ability to discuss a literary work with insight and understanding and to control a wide range of the elements of effective composition.

6-7   These papers also discuss symbolism in an appropriate novel or play. They discuss how symbolism evokes multiple meanings but are less thorough, less perceptive, or less specific than 8-9 papers. They deal with how symbolic meanings fit comfortably into the context of the story, but are less convincing than are the best responses. These essays are well-written, but with less maturity and control than the top papers. They demonstrate the writer's ability to analyze a literary work, but they reveal a more limited understanding than do papers scoring in the 8-9 range.

5   Superficiality characterizes these essays. They choose suitable settings, characters, actions, objects, motifs, or names, but their explanation of how these symbols are established by the author to evoke multiple meanings is vague or overly simplified. Their discussion of meaning may be pedestrian, mechanical or inadequately related to the chosen symbolism. Typically, these essays reveal simplistic thinking and/or immature writing. They usually demonstrate inconsistent control over the elements of composition and are not as well-conceived, organized, or developed as the upper-half papers. The writing, however, is sufficient to convey the writer's ideas.

3-4   These lower half essays may choose an acceptable work, but fail to explain how the author establishes symbols to evoke multiple responses. Their analysis of the importance of symbolism is likely to be unpersuasive, perfunctory, underdeveloped, or misguided. The meaning they adduce may be inaccurate or insubstantial and not clearly related to the chosen symbolism. Part of the question may be omitted altogether. The writing may convey the writer's ideas, but it reveals weak control over such elements as diction, syntax, organization, or grammar. Typically, these essays contain significant misinterpretations of the question or the work they discuss; they also may contain little, if any, supporting evidence, and practice paraphrase and plot summary at the expense of analysis.

1-2   The students who wrote these essays compound the weaknesses of the papers scoring in the 3-4 range. Theses writers seriously misread the play, novel, or poem, or seriously misinterpret the symbolism they have chosen. Frequently, they are unacceptably brief. Often poorly written on several counts, thee essays may contain many distracting errors in grammar and mechanics. Although some attempt may have been made to answer the question, the writer's views typically are presented with little clarity, organization, coherence, or supporting evidence.

PRACTICE TEST 1 SCORING

NOTE: See separate teacher's guide addendum for answers and explanations for all multiple-choice tests in this book. Add the results of your scores below to determine your AP Grade:

Section I: Multiple-Choice (Total)

_____ - (.25 X _____) = _____ X 1.2273=_____

| Number Correct | Number Wrong | Multiple-Choice Score | Weighted Score Section I |

Section II: Free-Response

Writing: Essay 1: _____ X 3.0556 = _____

Do not round

Writing: Essay 2: _____ X 3.0556 = _____

Do not round

Writing: Essay 3: _____ X 3.0556 = _____

Do not round

| Use CHECKLISTS or RUBRICS on the preceding pages to grade your essays. |

Weighted Section II Score

Do not round

Composite Score:

_____ + _____ = _____

| Weighted Multiple-Choice Score | Weighted Free-Response Score | **Composite** |

Composite Score	AP Grade
150 - 107 (71%)	5
106 - 93 (62%)	4
92 - 74 (49%)	3
73 - 44 (29%)	2
43 - 0	1

Practice Test 2:

Section 1
Multiple-
Choice

ENGLISH LITERATURE
AND COMPOSITION
SECTION I - Time -- 1 class period
Directions: This part consists of selections from prose works and questions on their content, form, and style. After reading each passage, choose the best answer to each question and completely fill in the corresponding oval on the answer sheet.
Note: Pay particular attention to the requirement of the questions that contain the words NOT, LEAST, or EXCEPT.

Questions 1 - 12. Read the following poem carefully before you choose your answers.

W. H. Auden

"The Unknown Citizen"

(To JS/07/M/373 This Marble Monument is Erected by the State)

He was found by the Bureau of Statistics to be
One against whom there was no official complaint,
And all the reports on his conduct agree
That, in the modern sense of an old-fashioned word, he was a saint,
(5)   For in everything he did he served the Greater Community.
Except for the war till the day he retired
He worked in a factory and never got fired, But satisfied his employers, Fudge Motors Inc.
Yet he wasn't a scab or odd in his views,
For his Union reports that he paid his dues,
(10)   (Our report on his Union shows it was sound)
And our Social Psychology workers found
That he was popular with his mates and liked a drink.
And that his reactions to poetry were normal in every way.

Policies taken out in his name prove that he was fully insured,

(15)   And his Health Card shows he was once in a hospital but left it cured.

Both Producers Research and High-Grade Living declare

He was fully sensible to the advantages of the Installment Plan

And had everything necessary to the Modern Man,

A gramophone, a radio, a car, and a Frigidaire.

(20)   Our researchers into public opinion are content

That he held the proper opinions for the time of year.

When there was peace, he was for peace; when there was war, he went.

He was married and added five children to the population,

Which our Eugenists say was the right number for a parent of his generation,

(25)   And our teachers report that he never interfered with their education.

Was he free? Was he happy? The question is absurd:

Had anything been wrong, we certainly should have heard.

1. All of the following beginning lines in the poem can be used to characterize Auden's style as exaggerant and smooth flowing EXCEPT:

> (A) "One against whom there was no official complaint"
> (B) "in the modern sense of an old-fashioned word, he was a saint"
> (C) "in everything he did he served the Greater Community"
> (D) "Except for the war till the day he retired"
> (E) "He worked in a factory and never got fired"

2. By using "the Bureau of Statistics" . . . "his Health Card" . . . "Producer's Research" and "Eugenists" the speaker seems to assume the audience is

> (A) fascinated about the realities of laborers
> (B) well-informed about the common man
> (C) obsessed with unknown citizens
> (D) interested in factual information
> (E) not acquainted with the unknown citizen

3. Which of the following does the author use as a synonym for society?

    (A) union

    (B) greater community   (D) fashionable society

    (C) eugenists   (E) commonwealth

4. In the passage, Fudge Motors, Inc., Eugenists, and teachers all share which of the following?

    (A) an ability to relate to the unknown citizen

    (B) an intense relationship in society

    (C) a concern with society's rules

    (D) a shallow satisfaction with the unknown citizen

    (E) a desire to encourage society

5. The speaker mentions that the unknown citizen "wasn't a scab" chiefly as a (an)

    (A) appeal to emotions

    (D) attempt at churlish indifference

    (C) attempt at folksiness

    (D) double entendre

    (E) illustration of inimitable eccentricity

6. The use of the phrase "Had anything been wrong, we certainly should have heard" has the effect of

    (A) clarifying the main point of the poem

    (B) characterizing the speaker as intentionally
        deceptive

    (C) repeating earlier references to being near perfect

    (D) exposing the speaker's controversial beliefs

    (E) forcing the reader to infer from earlier material
        what the phrase meant

7. Which of the following does the author use as a synonym for prevalent?

    (A) popular

    (B) decorous   (D) interfered

    (C) sensible   (E) proper

8. One of the goals of the poet in this poem was to

    (A) report events as objectively as possible

    (B) display knowledge of a regular citizen

    (C) discover meaning in apparent confusion

    (D) understand the basic humanity of the unknown
        citizen

    (E) confirm previous prejudices placed on the un-
        known citizen

9. The speaker's primary goal in the passage is to
    (A) use the events of the unknown citizen's life to generalize about other individuals
    (B) portray the imperfections and limitations of society
    (C) arose unrealistic and false expectations about the unknown citizen
    (D) convince the reader of the speaker's wisdom
    (E) tell about the happiness of the unknown citizen

10. All of the following are true about the unknown citizen EXCEPT:
    (A) He was a self-confident, outgoing person toward his fellow man.
    (B) His family was convinced that he bought a paper every day.
    (C) He was a very decorous, well-disposed person.
    (D) He was very truthful with all his colleagues.
    (E) He had no justifiable anger toward his fellow man.

11. The speaker of the poem can best be described as
    (A) an impartial observer
    (B) a sympathetic onlooker
    (C) an audacious visitor
    (D) a bemused apologist
    (E) a superficial bystander

12. The poet could have made the poem more derogatory in tone by
    (A) beginning the poem with negative descriptions
    (B) describing society's limitations in more detail
    (C) specifying how the unknown citizen acts
    (D) explaining the exact origin of society
    (E) concluding the passage with resentment

Questions 13-25. Read the following excerpt from *Emma*, a novel by Jane Austen, carefully before you choose your answers.

As Emma sat one morning, a note was brought from Mrs. Goddard requesting, in most respectful terms, to be allowed to bring Miss Smith with her; a most welcome request; for Miss Smith was a girl of seventeen, whom Emma knew very well by sight, and had long felt an interest in, on account of her beauty. A very gracious invitation was returned, and the evening no longer dreaded by the fair mistress of the mansion.

Harriet Smith was the natural* daughter of somebody.

Somebody had placed her, several years back, at Mrs. Goddard's school, and somebody had lately raised her from the condition of scholar to that of parlor border. This was all that was generally known of her history. She had no visible friends, but what had been acquired at Highbury, and was now just returned from a long visit in the country to some young ladies who had been at school there with her.

She was a very pretty girl, and her beauty happened to be of a sort which Emma particularly admired. She was short, plump, and fair, with a fine bloom, blue eyes, light hair, regular features, and a look of great sweetness; and, before the end of the evening, Emma was as much pleased with her manners as her person, and quite determined to continue the acquaintance.

She was not struck by anything remarkably clever in Miss Smith's conversation, but she found her altogether engaging — not inconveniently shy, nor unwilling to talk — and yet so far from pushing, showing so proper and becoming a deference, seeming so pleasantly grateful for being admitted to Hartfield, and so artlessly impressed by the appearance of everything in so superior a style to what she had been used to, that she must have good sense, and deserve encouragement. Encouragement should be given. Those soft blue eyes, and all those natural graces, should not be wasted on the inferior society of Highbury and its connections. The acquaintances she had already formed were unworthy of her. The friends from whom she had just parted, though very good sort of people, must be doing her harm. They were a family of the name of Martin, whom Emma well knew by character, as renting a large farm of Mrs. Knightley, and residing in the parish of Donwell — very creditably, she believed; she knew Mr. Knightley thought highly of them; but they must be coarse and unpolished, and very unfit to be the intimates of a girl who wanted only a little more knowledge and elegance to be quite perfect. She would notice her; she would improve her; she would detach her from her bad acquaintances, and introduce her into good society; she would form her opinions and her manners. It would be an interesting, and certainly a very kind undertaking; highly becoming her own situation in life, her leisure, and powers.

13. The author's primary purpose in this passage is to
>   (A) describe the effects of different events in Mrs. Goddard's life
>   (B) characterize the relationship between Mrs. Goddard and Mrs. Smith
>   (C) characterize Emma by her descriptions of why she likes Harriet
>   (D) depict Mrs. Goddard's enmity toward Harriet
>   (E) explain why Harriet was an illegitimate child

14. The blunt and brusque style of the passage can be seen in all of the following phrases EXCEPT:
>   (A) "She was short, plump, and fair."
>   (B) She had "blue eyes, light hair, regular features . . ."
>   (C) She was "a girl of seventeen . . . ."
>   (D) This was "a style to which she had been accustomed to . . ."
>   (E) "very good sort of people must be doing her harm . . ."

15. The phrases "Miss Smith was a girl of seventeen, whom Emma knew very well by sight, and had long felt an interest in, on account of her beauty" and "She was not struck by anything remarkably clever in Miss Smith's conversation" are similar in that each
>   (A) presents an image of Emma that she judges people by their outward appearance
>   (B) serves to undercut the character of Harriet in general
>   (C) repeats of qualifies the idea in the phrase that precedes it
>   (D) raises thought that Harriet is a very moral, unjudgmental person
>   (E) forces the reader to wait until the end to grasp the meaning of the characterization

16. All of the following are synonyms of the word "natural" as it is used by Jane Austen EXCEPT:
>   (A) illegitimate
>   (B) unrefined   (D) aberrant
>   (C) instinctive   (E) native

17. In the second paragraph, the narrator describes Harriet in order to aid the reader in
>   (A) becoming aware of Harriet's past
>   (B) developing a further characteristic of Emma
>   (C) hearing stories about Emma
>   (D) recognizing her earlier exposure to a harsh life
>   (E) becoming aware that Emma is trying to fit Harriet into Emma's society

18. All of the following indicate a portrayal of Emma, rather than Harriet EXCEPT:

    (A) "her beauty happened to be the sort which Emma particularly admired"

    (B) "Emma was much pleased with her manners"

    (C) "a note was brought requesting to bring Miss Smith with her"

    (D) "whom Emma knew very well by sight and had long felt an interest in"

    (E) "whom Emma knew well by character . . . very creditably . . ."

19. The main purpose of the third paragraph is to

    (A) generalize Harriet as a nice, smart girl

    (B) depict Harriet as a pretty, agreeable person

    (C) show that manners were important to Emma

    (D) show that Emma is a mild mannered person

    (E) show Emma uncertainty

20. All of the following oxymorons display Austen's ambiguous style EXCEPT:

    (A) "not inconveniently shy"

    (B) "pleasantly grateful"   (D) "inferior society"

    (C) "artlessly impressed"   (E) "harm(ful) friends"

21. All of the following could be synonyms for "deference" in the line "showing so proper . . . a deference" EXCEPT:

    (A) esteem

    (D) homage   (D) flippancy

    (C) honor   (E) respect

22. It can be inferred from the phrase "she found her altogether engaging — not inconveniently shy, nor unwilling to talk" that Emma

    (A) dreaded being alone

    (B) responded strongly but ambivalently to company

    (C) found Harriet's willingness to talk to be mystifying and unpleasant

    (D) was pleased with the friendliness of Harriet's character

    (E) was indifferent to the emotional force that lay behind Harriet's character

23. Which of the following describes Emma's character based on the line   "those natural graces, should not be wasted on the inferior society of Highbury and its connections" ?

    (A) haughty condescension

    (B) uninhibited passions   (D) awkwardness

    (C) misguided optimism   (E) duplicity

24. Emma defines Harriet's character in terms of which of the following aspects of her life?

    (A) Social

    (B) physical   (D) intellectual

    (C) financial   (E) spiritual

25. Which of the following phrases which end the passage indicates Emma's selfish motivation to make herself look good rather than a genuine effort to build a relationship?

    (A) "She found her altogether engaging."

    (B) "She must have good sense, and deserve encouragement."

    (C) She would detach her from her bad acquaintances, and introduce her into good society."

    (D) "She would form her opinions and her manners."

    (E) "It would be an interesting, and certainly a very kind undertaking, highly becoming her own situation in life."

<u>Questions 26-38.</u> Read the following poetic essay carefully before you choose your answers.

    I mention the spawning of toads because it is one of the phenomena of spring which mostly deeply appeal to me, and because the toad, unlike the skylark and the primrose, has never had much of a boost from the poets. But I am aware that many people do not like reptiles or amphibians, and I am not suggesting that in order to enjoy the spring you have to take an interest in toads. There are also the crocus, the missel thrush, the cuckoo, the blackthorn, etc. The point is that the pleasures of spring are available to everybody, and cost nothing. Even in the most sordid street the coming of spring will register itself by some sign or other, if it is only a brighter blue between the chimney pots or the vivid green of an elder sprouting on a blitzed site. Indeed it is remarkable how Nature goes on existing unofficially, as it were, in the very heart of London. I have seen a kestrel flying over the Deptford gasworks, and I have heard a first-rate performance by a blackbird in the Euston Road. There must be some hundreds of thousands, if not millions, of birds living inside the four-mile radius, and it is rather a pleasing thought that none of them pays a halfpenny for rent.

    As for spring, not even the narrow and gloomy streets round the Bank of England are quite able to exclude it. It comes seeping in everywhere, like one of those new poison gases which pass through all filters. The spring is commonly referred to as "a miracle," and during the past five or six years this worn-out figure of speech has taken on a new lease in life. After the sort of winters we have had to endure recently, the spring does seem miraculous, because it has become gradually harder and harder to believe that it is actually going to happen. Every February since 1940 I have found myself thinking that this time winter is going to be permanent. But Persephone, like the toads, always rises from the dead at about the same moment. Suddenly, towards the end of March, the miracle happens and the decaying slum in which I live is transfigured. Down in the square the sooty privets have turned bright green, the leaves are thickening on the chestnut trees, the daffodils are out, the wallflowers are budding, the policeman's tunic looks positively a pleasant shade of blue, the fishmonger greets his customers with a smile, and even the sparrows are quite a different color, having felt the balminess of the air and nerved themselves to take a bath, their first since last September.

26. In the phrase "the spawning of toads . . . is one of the phenomena of spring," the word "phenomena" can best be interpreted to mean

    (A) unusual occurrences

    (B) extraordinary eclipses   (D) scientific data

    (C) sense experiences   (E) common characteristics

27. Which of the following is the topic sentence that indicates the speaker's purpose for writing the first paragraph?

    (A) "I mention the spawning of toads because it is one of the phenomena of spring which mostly deeply appeal to me"

    (B) The spawning of toads . . . is one of the phenomena of spring which . . . has never had much of a boost from the poets."

    (C) "The pleasures of spring are available to everybody, and cost nothing. "

    (D) " Even in the most sordid street the coming of spring will register itself by some sign"

    (E) "It is remarkable how Nature goes on existing unofficially"

28. All of the following lines indicate supporting details for the topic sentence that indicates the speaker's purpose for writing the first paragraph EXCEPT:

    (A) "The coming of spring will register itself by . . .a brighter blue between the chimney pots"

    (B) " I have seen a kestrel flying over the Deptford gasworks"

    (C) "I have heard a first-rate performance by a blackbird in the Euston Road."

    (D) "There most be some hundreds of thousands, if not millions, of birds living inside the four--mile radius"

    (E) "It is rather a pleasing thought that none of (the birds) pays a halfpenny for rent"

29. What is the grammatical antecedent for the word "it" in the phrase "it is only a brighter blue between the chimney pots or the vivid green of an elder sprouting on a blitzed site" ?

    (A) the bright blue between chimney pots

    (B) vivid green of an elder sprouting

    (C) the coming of spring

    (D) the dramatic changes of nature

    (E) the sordid streets of London

30. The speaker in the first paragraph apparently assumes that the reader is

    (A) misinformed about spring

    (B) fascinated about the spawning of toads

    (C) interested in factual information

    (D) obsessed with the miracle of spring

    (E) concerned with the plight of kestrels

31. When the speaker in the first paragraph mentions "the Deptford gasworks" and "Euston Road," he apparently assumes the reader is

    (A) fascinated about winter

    (B) well-informed about London

    (C) obsessed with scientific methodology

    (D) yearning for the pleasures of springs

    (E) disgusted with the gloomy aspects of winter

32. The author is employing which of the following stylistic devices in the phrase "There must be some hundreds of thousands, if not millions, of birds living inside the four-mile radius" ?

    (A) allegory

    (B) anecdote   (D) hyperbole

    (C) parallelism   (E) onomatopoeia

33. Which of the following best describes the pattern of the author's discussion of spring in paragraph one?

      (A) statement of fact followed by tentative assumptions

      (B) descriptions of theory followed by exceptions to that theory

      (C) general statements followed by illustrative material

      (D) forceful argumentation followed by concessions to opponents

      (E) presentation of a problem followed by a solution to the problem

34. All of the following examples from paragraph one include common images associated with spring EXCEPT:

      (A) "The crocus, the missel thrush, the cuckoo, the blackthorn, etc."

      (B) " a brighter blue between the chimney pots"

      (C) "the vivid green of an elder sprouting "

      (D) "a kestrel* flying over the Deptford gasworks"

      (E) "a first-rate performance by a blackbird"

35. All of the following examples from paragraph two include rare images associated with spring EXCEPT:

      (A) "Down in the square the sooty privets have turned bright green"

      (B) "the leaves are thickening on the chestnut trees

      (C) " policeman's tunic looks positively a pleasant shade of blue"

      (D) "the fishmonger greets his customers with a smile"

      (E) "even the sparrows are quite a different color"

36. The primary purpose of the second paragraph seems to be to   (A) describe the miracle of spring

      (B) discuss the permanence of winter

      (C) tell the story of Persephone

      (D) forecast the balminess of the air

      (E) picture the thickening of the chestnut trees

37. The author's reference to Persephone is an example of using which stylistic device to help the reader see the change brought by the advent of spring?

      (A) syllogisms

      (B) allusions

      (C) authorial aside

      (D) balanced antithesis

      (E) compound sentences

38. The style of the passage as a whole can best be described
as   (A) abstract and allusive
       (B) disjointed and effusive
       (C) informal and descriptive
       (D) complex and pedantic
       (E) symbolic and terse

Questions 39-50. Read the following prose excerpt by Joseph
Conrad carefully before you choose your answers.

Captain MacWhirr, of the steamer Nan-Shan, had a physiognomy that, in order of material appearances, was the exact
counterpart of his mind: it presented no marked characteristics of firmness or stupidity; it had no pronounced characteristics whatever; it was simply ordinary, irresponsive, unruffled
. . . .

Having just enough imagination to carry him through
each successive day, and no more, he was tranquilly sure of
himself; and from the very same cause he was not in the least
conceited. It is your imaginative superior who is touchy, over-
bearing, and difficult to please; but every ship Captain
MacWhirr commanded was the floating abode of harmony and
peace. It was, in truth, as impossible for him to take a flight of
fancy as it would be for a watchmaker to put together a chro-
nometer with nothing except a two-pound hammer and a
whipsaw in the way of tools. Yet the uninteresting lives of
men so entirely given to the actuality of bare existence have
their mysterious side. It was impossible in Captain MacWhirr's
case, for instance, to understand what under heaven could have
induced that perfectly satisfactorily son of a petty grocer in
Belfast to run away to sea. And yet he had done that very
thing at the age of fifteen. It was enough, when you thought it
over, to give you an idea of the immense, potent, and visible
hand thrust into the ant-heap of the earth, laying hold of shoulders, knocking heads together, and setting the unconscious
faces of the multitude towards inconceivable goals and in un-
dreamt-of directions.

His father never really forgave him for his undutiful
stupidity. "We could have got on without him," he used to say
later on, "but there's the business. And he an only son, too!"
His mother wept very much after his disappearance. As it
never occurred to him to leave word behind, he was mourned
over for dead till, after eight months, his first letter arrived
from Talcahuano. It was short, and contained the statement:
"We had very fine weather on our passage out." But evidently,

in the writer's mind, the only important intelligence was to the effect that his captain had, on the very day of writing, entered him regularly on the ship's articles as Ordinary Seaman. "Because I can do the work," he explained. The mother wept copiously, while the remark, "Tom's an ass," expressed the emotions of the father. He was a corpulent man, with a gift for sly chaffing, which to the end of his life he exercised in his intercourse with his son, a little pityingly, as if upon a half-witted person.

MacWhirr's visits to his home were necessarily rare, and in the course of years he dispatched other letters to his parents, informing them of his successive promotions and of his movements upon the vast earth. In these missives could be found sentences like this: "The heat here is very great." Or: "On Christmas Day at 4 PM. we fell in with some icebergs." The old people ultimately became acquainted with a good many names of ships, and with the names of the skippers who commanded them — with the names of Scots and English ship-owners — with the names of seas, oceans, straits, promonto-ries — with outlandish names of lumber-ports, of rice-ports, of cotton-ports — with the names of islands — with the names of their son's young woman. She was called Lucy. It did not suggest itself to him to mention whether he thought the name pretty. And then they died.

39. The word "physiognomy," in the context of the first para-graph, can be defined as the practice of judging
        (A) mental qualities by observations of bodily features
        (B) facial features by the person's bodily expressions
        (C) outward appearances as an indication of the soundness of the anatomy
        (D) the constitution of the body by physical mannerisms
        (E) inner emotions by the observations of thoughts

40. Which of the following is the antecedent of "him" in "it was . . . impossible for him to take a flight of fancy" ?
        (A) Nan-Shan
        (B) Father
        (C) Tom
        (D) Captain MacWhirr
        (E) Ordinary Seamen

41. All of the following are euphemisms or kind phrases chosen by Conrad to describe Captain MacWhirr's boring personality EXCEPT:

    (A) "It presented no marked characteristics of firm-
        ness"
    (B) "It had no pronounced characteristics whatsoever"
    (C) "stupidity"
    (D) "irresponsive"
    (E) "unruffled"

42. Even though the Captain was a boring personality, he was
described paradoxically as

    (A) "having just enough imagination to carry him
        through the day"
    (B) "being "tranquilly sure of himself"
    (C) "touchy, overbearing, and difficult to please"
    (D) one who ran "away to sea . . . at the age of fifteen"
    (E) "a half-witted person"

43. When Conrad tries to help us understand the power of the
action taken by Captain MacWhirr in running away from home,
he compares it to a "potent, and visible hand thrust into the
ant-heap of the earth, laying hold of shoulders, knocking heads
together, and setting the unconscious faces of the multitude
towards unconceivable goals and in un-dreamt-of directions."
This type of comparison is called a

    (A) metaphor
    (B) hyperbole   (D) antithesis
    (C) parallelism   (E) command

44. Which of the following best describes the tone of Conrad's
voice when he says "His father never really forgave him for
his undutiful stupidity"?

    (A) comical
    (B) fascinated   (D) sarcastic
    (C) empathetic   (E) coldhearted

45. Captain MacWhirr left home, breaking all ties with his
family, because his father was

    (A) "a corpulent man"
    (B) gifted in "sly chaffing"
    (C) "a half-witted person"
    (D) interested in the names of Scots and English
        shipowners
    (E) mad at his wife Lucy

46. All of the following are examples of Joseph Conrad's gift of conciseness EXCEPT:

    (A) "Every ship Captain MacWhirr commanded was the floating abode of harmony and peace."

    (B) "The uninteresting lives of men so entirely given to the actuality of bare existence have their mysterious side."

    (C) "It was impossible . . . to understand what under heaven could have induced that perfectly satisfactory son of a petty grocer in Belfast to run away at sea."

    (D) "His father never really forgave him for his undutiful stupidity."

    (E) "We had very fine weather on our passing out."

47. Which of the following is an example of Conrad's use of a simile?

    (A) "From the very same cause he was not in the least conceited."

    (B) It was . . . as impossible for him to take flight of fancy as it would be for a watchmaker to put together a chronometer with nothing but a two pound hammer and a whipsaw . . . for tools."

    (C) "We could have gone without him," he used to say later on, "but there's the business."

    (D) In these missives could be found sentences like this: "The heat here is very great."

    (E) "It did not suggest to him to mention whether he thought the name pretty."

48. The contrast between Captain MacWhirr and his father emphasizes MacWhirr's

    (A) defenselessness and the father's lack of compassion

    (B) self-confidence and the father's lack of knowledge

    (C) innocence and the father's justified anger

    (D) sense of humor and the father's resentment

    (E) ability to retaliate and the father's lack of wit

49. The rhetorical strategy of the last sentence, "And then they died," can best be described as

    (A) conclude the sketch with an expected tragedy

    (B) reduce the argument to an acceptable paradox

    (C) marshal facts to support the main idea

    (D) make an abstraction concrete with an analogy

    (E) counterbalance a possible weakness with a stronger virtue

Practice Test 2:
"Use A PEN"

ENGLISH
LITERATURE AND COMPOSITION
SECTION II
Time — 2 hours
Number of questions — 3
Percent of total grade — 55

Question I
(Suggested time — 40 minutes. This question
counts one-third of the total)

Prior to the beginning of the following excerpt from "Story of an Hour," great care has been taken to break to Mrs. Mallard the news that her husband had been killed in a car accident. As the story progresses, Kate Chopin, the author, seems to sympathize with Mrs. Mallard, despite the fact that her grieving over her husband's death is mixed with joy. Read the short story carefully. Then write a well-organized essay in which you analyze how Chopin uses such resources of language as descriptive diction, imagery, and figurative language to convey her attitude toward Mrs. Mallard.

She sat with her head thrown back upon the cushion of the chair, quite motionless, except when a sob came up into her throat and shook her, as a child who has cried itself to sleep continues to sob in its dreams.

She was young, with a fair, calm face, whose lines bespoke repression and even a certain strength. But now there was a dull stare in her eyes, whose gaze was affixed away off yonder on one of those patches of blue sky. It was not a glance of reflection, but rather indicated a suspension of intelligent thought.

There was something coming to her and she was waiting for it, fearfully. What was it? She did not know; it was too subtle and elusive to name. But she felt it, creeping out of the sky, reaching toward her through the sounds, the scents, the color that filled the air.

Now her bosom rose and fell tumultuously. She was beginning this thing that was approaching to possess her, and she was striving to beat it back with her will — as powerless as her two white slender hands would have been.

When she abandoned herself a little whispered word escaped her slightly parted lips. She said it over and over under her breath: "free, free, free!" The vacant stare and the look of terror that had followed it went with her eyes. They stayed keen and bright. Her pulses beat fast, and the coursing blood warmed and relaxed every inch of her body.

She did not stop to ask if it were or were not a monstrous joy that held her. A clear and exalted perception enabled her to dismiss the suggestion as trivial.

She knew that she would weep again when she saw the kind, tender hands folded in death; the face that had never looked save with love upon her, fixed and gray and dead. But she saw beyond that bitter moment a long procession of years to come that would belong to her absolutely. And she opened and spread her arms out to them in welcome.

There would be no one to live for during those coming years; she would live for herself. There would be no powerful will bending hers in that blind persistence with which men and women believe they have a right to impose a private will upon a fellow-creature. A kind intention or a cruel intention made the act seem no less a crime as she looked upon it in that brief moment of illumination. . . .

Josephine was kneeling before the closed door with her lips to the keyhole imploring for admission. . . .

"Go away. I am not making myself ill." No; she was drinking in a very elixir of life through that open window. . . .

She arose at length and opened the door to her sister's importunities. There was a feverish triumph in her eyes, and she carried herself unwittingly like a goddess of Victory. She clasped her sister's waist, and together they descended the stairs. Richards stood waiting for them at the bottom.

Someone was opening the front door with a latchkey. It was Brently Mallard who entered, a little travel-stained, composedly carrying his gripsack and umbrella. He had been far from the scene of the accident, and did not even know there had been one. He stood amazed at Josephine's piercing cry; at Richard's quick motion to screen him from the view of his wife.

But Richard's was too late.

When the doctors came they said she had died of heart disease — of joy that kills.

Question 2
(Suggested time — 40 minutes. This question counts one-third of the total essay score.)

Read carefully the following poem by American poet, Emily Dickinson. Then write a well-organized essay in which you discuss how the central metaphor of stanzas two and three express the complex attitude of the speaker.

> *I dwell in Possibility* —

> I dwell in Possibility —
> A fairer House than Prose —
> More numerous of Windows —
> Superior — for Doors —

(5)   Of Chambers as the Cedars —
> Impregnable of Eye —
> And for an Everlasting Roof —
> The Gambrels of the Sky —

> Of Visitors — the fairest —
(10)   For Occupation — This —
> The spreading wide my narrow Hands
> To gather Paradise —

Question 3
(Suggested time — 40 minutes. This questions counts
one-third of the total essay score.)

Some workers select unreliable narrators, whose interpretations of events are different from those of the author's. Select a work of literary merit in which the narrator, perhaps because of youth, lack of self knowledge, or lack of sophistication, could be considered unreliable. Then analyze how the choice of narration is artistically appropriate for the author's purpose.

Choose a novel by one of the following authors or another author of comparable merit.

Mark Twain	Chinua Achebe
Charles Dickens	James Baldwin
Harper Lee	Saul Bellow
J. D. Salinger	Joseph Conrad
Ralph Ellison	Zora Neal Hurston
Toni Morrison	Eudora Welty
Alice Walker	Virginia Woolf
Willa Cather	Richard Wright
Margaret Atwood	John Updike
Louise Erdich	Bernard Malamud
William Faulkner	F. Scot Fitzgerald

Answers and Explanations

To Practice Test 2: Section II: Essay

Checklist for
Question 1
from Kate Chopin's "Story of an Hour"

STEP 1:   Check each item listed below which accurately describes the positive aspects of the essay being graded. Add one point for each item checked from the list. This side describes the basic requirements for a well-written essay. (Grader one should check column one. Grader two should check column two):

___-___1. The writer demonstrates an awareness of the complexity of Chopin's attitude toward Mrs. Mallard, including a discussion of its irony.

___-___2. The writer analyzes how descriptive diction, imagery, and figurative language distinguish Chopin's attitude toward Mrs. Mallard.

___-___3. The thesis clearly shows the connection between Chopin's attitude toward Mrs. Mallard and the language devices used to convey that attitude.

___-___4. The writer makes apt (a minimum of three embedded bits of quotes per paragraph) and specific (detailed and appropriate) reference to the text.

___-___5. The writer offers a convincing interpretation of the irony of Chopin's sympathetic attitude toward Mrs. Mallard.

___-___6. The writer demonstrates an ability to read perceptively by saying something beyond the easy and obvious to grasp

___-___7. The writer demonstrates a control over the virtues of effective communication, including the language unique to literary criticism.

___-___8. The writer's organization is implicit and original, yet communicates a clear message.

___-___9. The writer's diction, sentence structure, and grammar aid in communicating a clear message.

MAXIMUM SCORE RESULTS: Grader 1 _____

MAXIMUM SCORE RESULTS: Grader 2 _____

STEP 2:   Check each item below which accurately describes the negative aspects of the essay being graded. This side describes how the essay may not be as good as the higher-scoring essays. (Grader one should check column one. Grader two should check column two):

___-___1. The writer's definition of the attitude is oversimplified or vague or omits any discussion of its irony.

___-___2. The writer discusses the rhetorical and stylistic devices with limited purpose or with inappropriate examples.

___-___3. The connection between the evidence and the author's attitude is less clear than those of the top-scoring essays.

___-___4. The writer's use of quotes is awkward, inappropriate, or uninteresting.

___-___5. The writer misreads the meaning of the passage or simply paraphrases the passage with no reference to the language devices used.

___-___6. The writer's interpretation is not as persuasive as those of the highest scoring essays.

___-___7. The writer misuses the literary term(s) addressed in the question or omits them partially or entirely.

___-___8. The organization of this essay is less original or implicit than those of the top-scoring essays.

___-___9. The essay reveals consistent weakness in grammar and/or other basic elements of composition.

RESULTS:

Grader 1: _____ - _____ = _____
             Step 1 Score   Step 2 Score

Grader 2: _____ - _____ = _____
             Step 1 Score   Step 2 Score

Grader 1 Score + Grader 2 Score = _____

Above sum /
divided by 2 =

Score for essay

Answers and Explanations

To Practice Test 4:
Section II: AP Rubrics

Rubrics for Question 1

from Kate Chopin's "Story of an Hour"

8-9   Students who wrote essays earning a score of 8-9 show a clear understanding of how Chopin's use of the language and rhetorical devices reflect her sympathetic attitude toward Mrs. Mallard. The writer presents a clear and relevant thesis — correctly identifying the irony of Chopin's attitude — supported by apt and specific evidence from the passage. The organization of these high scoring-essays is implicit and clear. Thoroughly convincing, this prose demonstrates the writer's ability to control a wide range of the elements of effective writing, including the language unique to literary criticism, but need not be without flaws.

6-7   Students who wrote essays earning the score of 6-7 correctly identify Chopin's attitude and analyze adequately how she conveys that ironic view, but the thesis is less specific than the top-scoring essays. Typically they show how some language or rhetorical devices convey that view, but leave out at least one important element, making the evidence less convincing. The connection between the evidence and Chopin's attitude may also be less clear than the top-scoring essays. The organization is less implicit than those of the highest-scoring essays. A few lapses in diction, syntax, or use of literary language may be present, but usually the prose of essays scoring a 6 convey their writers' ideas clearly.

5   Students who wrote essays earning the score of 5 define Chopin's attitude, but do not address the irony implicit in the passage. Their analysis of how she conveys that view, while accurate, is also limited or inconsistently developed. The writer may simply name the attitude without discussing it or he/she may not aptly address the language or rhetorical devices Chopin uses to convey that mood. The thesis may be too simple or the evidence too brief to prove the writer's points. The organization follows a typical five paragraph model. A few lapses in diction or syntax may be present, but for the most part, the prose of essays scoring a 5 conveys their writers' ideas clearly.

3-4   Students who wrote essays earning the score of 3-4 may not answer the entire question. Frequently they misrepresent Chopin's attitude, analyze stylistic elements with limited purpose or accuracy, or catalogue various stylistic elements in the passage without relating them to Chopin's attitude. The prose of essays scoring a 4 usually conveys their writers' ideas adequately, but may suggest inconsistent control over such elements of writing as literary language, organization, diction, and syntax.

1-2   Students who wrote essays earning the score of 1-2 demonstrate little or no success in characterizing Chopin's view and in analyzing how it is conveyed. Some substitute a simpler task, such as paraphrasing the passage or discussing language and rhetorical elements in general. The paper may be unusually short and the prose of essays scoring a 2 may reveal consistent weakness in grammar or another of the basic elements of composition.

Answers and Explanations
To Practice Test 3:
Section II: Results
of Essay 3

Kate Chopin's "Story of an Hour"

Following are examples of how the writer may demonstrate an awareness of the complexity of Chopin's attitude toward Mrs. Mallard, including a discussion of its irony.

> A. Grief is a personal, unique and all-together terrifyingly complex emotion.
> B. In this essay by Kate Chopin, it seems quite ironic that Mrs. Mallard's grieving is mixed with some joy.
> C. In Chopin's passage, a wife's cycle of grieving is chronicled by an ironically sympathetic author.

Following are examples of how the writer may analyze how the resources of language distinguish Chopin's attitude toward Mrs. Mallard. Besides descriptive diction, imagery, and figurative language some students picked other devices such as point of view, similes and pathos, but the important thing is to connect language back to the focus of the question. That is, connect the author's manipulation of the language to the creation of the attitude.

> A. "Chopin's ironically sympathetic attitude can be seen through her use of similes. (This gets a check but it is less perceptive than those of the higher scoring essays so it would also get a check on the left. In fact, if you use this organizational approach, the highest you will probably score is a 6)
> B. Kate Chopin sympathizes with Mrs. Mallard against marriage and the "persistence" with which it "imposes" on men and women. (The approach in B and C connects language to meaning in a more natural way, resulting in a higher score.)
> C. Describing Mrs. Mallard in terms contradictory to what is expected for a grieving widow creates a hidden irony.

The writer also must make apt (a minimum of three embedded bits of quotes per paragraph) and specific (detailed and appropriate) reference to the text.

A. The "feverish triumph" in her eyes and the "brief moment of illumination" she felt, set her outside the reality of this moment.

Following are examples of how the writer could offer a convincing interpretation of the irony of Chopin's sympathetic attitude toward Mrs. Mallard.

A. Kate Chopin describes a woman who, at the height of her grief, can not decipher whether it is joy or sorrow she is feeling.

B. Although both grief-stricken and joyful, the author seems to admire Mrs. Mallard's independence.

Following are examples of how the writer could demonstrate an ability to read perceptively by saying something beyond the easy and obvious to grasp.

A. Somewhere the writer must mention how the empathy toward Mrs. Mallard sets the reader up for the surprise ending.

B. The metaphors present are positive, uplifting, and have nothing to do with death.

The writer must demonstrate a control over the virtues of effective communication, including the language unique to literary criticism. Correct the following misuse of literary terms:

A. Kate Chopin picks descriptive terms contrary to the **genre** of a funeral day.

B. The author uses **allusion** to show how Mrs. Mallard sees things that are not there.

The writer's organization should be implicit and original, yet communicate a clear message. The highest score will discuss the language of the passage in a natural way. Do not force the same organization into every essay. Topic sentences, like those below, that name the device and make a connection to the attitude, yet say nothing specific SHOULD BE AVOIDED:

A. The imagery shows the irony in the story.

B. Chopin's sympathy is shown through her use of similes.

The writer's diction, sentence structure, and grammar need to aid in communicating a clear message. Correct the following:

A. After receiving news of his death there was a vacant feeling in her being.

B. I will use descriptive diction, imagery, and figurative language to prove to you that Kate Chopin felt sympathy for Mrs. Mallard.

Answers and Explanations

To Practice Test 2:
Section II: Essay
Question 2

Checklist for Question 1   from "I dwell in Possibility"
by Emily Dickinson

STEP 1:   Check each item listed below which accurately describes the positive aspects of the essay being graded. Add one point for each item checked from the list. This side describes the basic requirements for a well-written essay. (Grader one should check column one. Grader two should check column two):

___-___1. The writer demonstrates a thorough understanding of the speaker's complex attitude toward poetry.

___-___2. The writer analyzes how the poem's central metaphor expresses the speaker's complex attitude.

___-___3. The writer makes apt and specific references to "I dwell in Possibility."

___-___4. The writer offers a convincing interpretation of "I dwell in Possibility."

___-___5. The writer demonstrates an ability to read perceptively by making conclusions that are beyond the obvious and easy to grasp.

___-___6. This essay adequately supports the discussion of each language device by using a minimum of three embedded bits of quotes per paragraph.

___-___7. The writer demonstrates the hall marks of good writing by communicating a clear message through the use of implicit organization.

___-___8. The writer demonstrates consistent control over the language unique to the criticism of literature.

___-___9. The diction, sentence structure, and grammar also aid in communicating a clear message.

MAXIMUM SCORE RESULTS: Grader 1 _____
MAXIMUM SCORE RESULTS: Grader 2 _____

STEP 2:   Check each item below which accurately describes the negative aspects of the essay being graded. This side describes how the essay may not be as good as the higher-scoring essays. (Grader one should check column one. Grader two should check column two):

___-___1. The writer's handling of the complex attitude of the speaker is less thorough or less precise than those of the higher scoring essays

___-___2. The writer's discussion of how the poem's central metaphor expresses the speaker's complex attitude is more vague, mechanical and briefer than those of the higher scoring essays.

___-___3. The writer's analysis is less well-supported and less incisive than those of the higher scoring essays.

___-___4. The writer's analysis has minor flaws in interpretation.

___-___5. The writer misses the complexity of Dickinson's poem.

___-___6. Although adequate in number, the evidence in this essay is not as convincing as the top-scoring essay.

___-___7. A few lapses in language unique to literary criticism may be present, but the message is clear.

___-___8. The organization of this essay is less appropriate than those of the top-scoring essays.

___-___9. The essay reveals consistent weakness in grammar and/or other basic elements of composition.

RESULTS:

Grader 1: _____ - _____ = _____
           Step 1 Score   Step 2 Score

Grader 2: _____ - _____ = _____
           Step 1 Score   Step 2 Score

Grader 1 Score + Grader 2 Score = _____

Above sum /
divided by 2 =

Score for essay

Answers and Explanations

To Practice Test 2:
Section II: AP Rubrics

Rubrics for Question 2

from Emily Dickinson's "I dwell in Possibility"

8-9   The students who wrote these essays clearly demonstrate an understanding of how the poem's central metaphor expresses the complex attitude of the speaker. In their references, they are apt and specific. Though not without flaws, these papers will offer a convincing interpretation of "I dwell in Possibility" and consistent control over the elements of effective composition. They demonstrate the writer's ability to write with clarity and skill.

6-7   The students who wrote these essays also demonstrate an understanding of Dickinson's poem; but, compared to the best essays, they are less thorough or less precise in their analysis of how the controlling metaphor expresses the complex attitude of the speaker. In addition to minor flaws in interpretation, their discussion is likely to be less well supported and less incisive. These essays demonstrate the writer's ability to express ideas clearly, but with less mastery and control than the 8-9 papers.

5   The substance of essays scoring a 5 are characterized by superficiality. Their discussion of how the controlling metaphor expresses the complex attitude of the speaker may be vague, mechanical, or inadequately supported. They deal with the assigned tasks without important errors, but miss the complexity of Dickinson's poem. The writing is sufficient to convey the writer's thoughts, but these essays are typically pedestrian, not as well conceived, organized or developed as the upper-half papers. Often they reveal simplistic thinking and/or immature writing.

3-4   These lower half essays often reflect an incomplete or oversimplified understanding of the poem. Typically, they fail to respond to part(s) of the question. Their discussion may be meager, weak, or irrelevant. The controlling metaphor is insufficiently identified, or the issues of complexity incompletely grasped; the discussion inaccurate or unclear. The writing demonstrates shaky control over the standard elements of college-level composition. These essays usually contain recurrent stylistic flaws and/or misreadings, and they often lack of persuasive evidence from the text.

1-2 These essay compound the weaknesses of the 3-4 range. They are marred by many inaccuracies: significant misinterpretations, insufficient development, and serious omissions. Frequently they are unacceptably brief. They are often poorly written on several counts and may contain many distracting errors in grammar and mechanics. While some attempt has been made to answer the question, the writer's views are presented with little clarity.

0   This is a response with no more than a reference to the poem.

- Indicates a blank response, or is completely off the topic.

Answers and Explanations

To Practice Test 2:
Section II: Results
of Essay 2

Question 1
from "I dwell in Possibility"
by Emily Dickinson

Following are examples of how the writer may demonstrate a thorough understanding of how the controlling metaphor expresses the speaker's complex attitude:

> A. In the first two lines of the poem, the speaker names the house as a metaphor expressing the speaker's ambiguous preference for poetry over prose.
>
> B. The imagery employed throughout the poem compares poetry to prose as though they both were houses, each having their own windows, doors, chambers and roofs, but the house of poetry has more "possibilities."
>
> C. The imagery of the house progresses from comparisons of man made objects to nature objects to supernatural objects

Following are examples of how the writer could make apt and specific references (a minimum of three embedded bits of quotes per paragraph) to "I dwell in Possibility," offering a convincing interpretation of the poem's meaning that demonstrates an ability to read perceptively by making conclusions that are beyond the obvious and easy to grasp:

> A. The Chambers of the house of poetry are made of "Cedar," known for it beauty, fragrance, and durability. It is "Impregnable of Eye --"
>
> B. The roof of the house of poetry is compared to the sky, but the qualifier, "Everlasting," raise it even higher.
>
> C. In the final two line the poet's comparison becomes even more expansive. She is able to spread wide her "narrow Hands/To Gather Paradise."

D. The house of Poetry is a better house because it offers more "Possibility" in the form of more numerous . . . windows . . . Doors . . . " and an "Everlasting Roof."

Correct the following mistakes in diction, sentence structure, or grammar:

A. There are many interpretations of the value of poetry in today's society.

B. Imagery is continuously used throughout the poem to convey meaning.

C. Within Dickinson's poem, the reader is drawn by his unique choice of words, and in this can take normal every day diction and produce a kaleidoscope of meanings

D. In the poem "I dwell in Possibility" by Dickinson, many different ideas and definitions are thrown out for the reader to grasp.

E. The order in which Dickinson writes the poem is very jumpy.

Answers and Explanations

To Practice Test 2:
Section II: Essay

Checklist for
Question 3

Open Question on NAIVELY NARRATED NOVELS

STEP 1: Check each item listed below which accurately describes the positive aspects of the essay being graded. Add one point for each item checked from the list. This side describes the basic requirements for a well-written essay. (Grader one should check column one. Grader two should check column two):

___-___1. The writer selects a suitable novel in which the narrator is considered to be unreliable.

___-___2. The writer presents a reasonable explanation of the purpose and meaning of the work.

___-___3. The writer effectively explains how the narrator's youth, lack of self-knowledge, or lack of sophistication makes him/her an unreliable narrator, whose interpretations are different from those of the author.

___-___4. The writer effectively explains how the choice of narration is artistically appropriate for the author's purpose.

___-___5. The writer makes apt and specific reference to the text.

___-___6. The writer avoids plot summary not relevant to the explanation of the role that narrator plays in telling the story.

___-___7. The writer discusses the literary work with sophistication, insight, and understanding.

___-___8. The writer's displays consistent control over the language unique to the discussion of narration.

___-___9. The writer's diction, sentence structure, organization, and grammar aid in communicating a clear message.

MAXIMUM SCORE RESULTS: Grader 1 _____

MAXIMUM SCORE RESULTS: Grader 2 _____

STEP 2:   Check each item below which accurately describes the negative aspects of the essay being graded. This side describes how the essay may not be as good as the higher-scoring essays. (Grader one should check column one.   Grader two should check column two):

___-___1. The writer's selection of a naively narrated novel is not as appropriate as those of the higher scoring essays.

___-___2. The writer's explanation of the meaning of the work is less thorough, less specific, or less perceptive than those of the higher scoring essays.

___-___3. The writer's explanation of how the narrator's youth, lack of self-knowledge, or lack of sophistication makes him/her an unreliable narrator, whose interpretations are different from those of the author, may be vague, underdeveloped, or misguided.

___-___4. The writer's explanation of how the choice of narration is artistically appropriate for the author's purpose may be less convincing, mechanical, or inadequately related to the work as a whole.

___-___5. The writer's reference to the text lack the specificity of the higher scoring essays.

___-___6. The writer simply paraphrases the meaning of the work with little reference to its symbolic significance.

___-___7. The writer says nothing beyond the easy and obvious to grasp.

___-___8. The writer misuses the literary term(s) necessary to the discussion of narration or omits them partially or entirely.

___-___9. The essay contains distracting errors in grammar and mechanics.   RESULTS:

Grader 1: _____ - _____ = _____

          Step 1 Score   Step 2 Score

Grader 2: _____ - _____ = _____

          Step 1 Score   Step 2 Score

Grader 1 Score + Grader 2 Score = _____

Above sum /
divided by 2 =

Score for essay

Answers and Explanations

To Practice Test 2:
Section II: AP Rubrics

Rubrics for Question 3

Free Response on NAIVELY NARRATED NOVELS

8-9   The students who wrote these well-written essays choose a suitable novel in which the narrator is considered to be unreliable, and they explain convincingly how the narrator functions in the work.   Superior papers will be specific in their references, cogent in their explications, and free of plot summary not directly relevant to the role that narration plays in the work. These essays may not be flawless, but they demonstrate the writer's ability to discuss a literary work with insight and understanding and to control a wide range of the elements of effective composition.

6-7   These essays also analyze an appropriate naive narrator from an acceptable work of literature; they discuss how the narrator's youth, lack of knowledge, or lack of sophistication makes him/her an unreliable narrator, but are less thorough, less perceptive, or less specific than 8-9 papers. They deal with how the choice of narration is artistically appropriate for the author's purpose, but are less convincing than are the best responses. These essays are well written, but with less maturity and control than the top papers. They demonstrate the writer's ability to analyze a literary work, but they reveal a more limited understanding than do papers scoring an 8 or 9.

5   Superficiality characterizes these essays. They choose suitable narrators, but their explanation of how the choice of narration is artistically appropriate for the author's purpose is vague or oversimplified. Their discussion of meaning may be pedestrian, mechanical or inadequately related to the chosen symbolism. Typically, these essays reveal simplistic thinking and/or immature writing. They usually demonstrate inconsistent control over the elements of composition and are not as well conceived, organized, or developed as the upper-half papers. The writing, however, is sufficient to convey the writer's ideas.

3-4   These lower-half essays may choose an acceptable work, but fail to explain how the author's choice of narration affects the work. Their analysis of the importance of the naive narrator is likely to be unpersuasive, perfunctory, underdeveloped, or misguided. The meaning they adduce may be inaccurate or insubstantial and not clearly related to the chosen narrator. Part of the question may be omitted altogether. The writing may convey the writer's ideas, but it reveals weak control over such elements as diction, syntax, organization, or grammar. Typically, these essays contain significant misinterpretations of the question or the work they discuss; they also may contain little, if any, supporting evidence, and practice paraphrase and plot summary at the expense of analysis.

1-2   These essays compound the weaknesses of the papers scoring a 3 or 4. The writers seriously misread the novel, or seriously misinterpret the significance of the naive narrator's role. Frequently, they are unacceptably brief. Often poorly written on several counts, these essays may contain many distracting errors in grammar and mechanics. Although some attempt may have been made to answer the question, the writer's views typically are presented with little clarity, organization, coherence, or supporting evidence.

PRACTICE TEST 2 SCORING

NOTE: See separate teacher's guide for answers and explanations for all multiple-choice tests in this book. Add the results of your scores below to determine your AP Grade:

Section I: Multiple-Choice (Total)

_____ - (.25 X _____) = _____ X 1.2273=_____

| Number Correct | Number Wrong | Multiple-Choice Score | Weighted Score Section I |

Section II: Free-Response

Writing: Essay 1: _____ X 3.0556 = _____

Do not round

Writing: Essay 2: _____ X 3.0556 = _____

Do not round

Writing: Essay 3: _____ X 3.0556 = _____

Do not round

Use CHECKLISTS or RUBRICS on the preceding pages to grade your essays.

Weighted Section II Score

Do not round

Composite Score:

_____ + _____ = _____

Weighted Multiple- Choice Score   Weighted Free- Response Score   **Composite**

Composite Score	AP Grade
150 - 107 (71%)	5
106 - 93 (62%)	4
92 - 74 (49%)	3
73 - 44 (29%)	2
43 - 0	1

Practice Test 3:

General Instructions

ENGLISH LITERATURE
AND COMPOSITION

Three hours are allotted for this examination: 1 hour for Section I, which consists of multiple-choice questions, and 2 hours for Section II, which consists of essay questions. The multiple-choice questions are printed in this booklet. All essay questions are printed in a separate green booklet.

SECTION I

Time — 1 hour
Number of questions — 50
Percent of total grade — 45
This examination contains 50 multiple-choice questions. Therefore, please be careful to fill in only the ovals that are preceded by numbers 1 through 50 on your answer sheet.

General Instructions

DO NOT OPEN THIS TEST BOOKLET UNTIL YOU ARE INSTRUCTED TO DO SO.

INDICATE ALL YOUR ANSWERS TO QUESTIONS IN SECTION I ON THE SEPARATE ANSWER SHEET.   No credit will be given for anything written in this examination booklet, but you may use the booklet for notes or scratch work. After you have decided which of the suggested answers is best, COMPLETELY fill in the corresponding oval on the answer sheet. Give only one answer to each question. If you change an answer, be sure that the previous mark is erased completely.

Example: <u>Sample Answer:</u>

 Eagle Pass is a   A Ⓐ C D E

 (A) state
 (B) city
 (C) country
 (D) continent
 (E) village

Many candidates wonder whether or not to guess on the answers to questions about which they are not certain. In this section of the examination, as a correction for haphazard guessing, one-fourth of the number of questions you answer incorrectly will be subtracted from the questions you answer correctly. It is improbable, therefore, that mere guessing will improve your score significantly; it may even lower your score, and it does take time. If, however, you are not sure of the correct answer but have some knowledge of the question and are able to eliminate one or more of the answer choices as wrong, your chance of getting the right answer is improved, and it may be to your advantage to answer such a question.

Use your time effectively, working as rapidly as you can without losing accuracy. Do not spend too much time on questions that are too difficult. Go on to other questions and come back to the difficult ones later if you have time. It is not expected that everyone will be able to answer all the multiple-choice questions.

Note: These directions are copied from the multiple-choice section of *The 1991 Advanced Placement Examination in English Literature and Composition and Its Grading.*   Princeton, New Jersey: Educational Testing Service, 1993.

Practice Test 3:

General Instructions

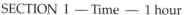

ENGLISH LITERATURE
AND COMPOSITION
MULTIPLE CHOICE
          SECTION I — Time — 1 hour

<u>Directions:</u> This section consists of literary works and questions on their content, form, and style. After reading each passage, choose the best answer to each question and fill in the corresponding oval on the answer sheet.

Note: Pay particular attention to the requirements of questions that contain the words NOT, LEAST, or EXCEPT.

<u>Questions 1-13.</u> Read the following excerpt from Edgar Allan Poe's short story, "The Tell-Tale Heart" carefully before choosing your answers.

          TRUE! — nervous — very, very dreadfully nervous I had been and am; but why will you say that I am mad? The disease had sharpened my senses — not destroyed — not dulled them. Above all was the sense of hearing acute. I heard all things in the heaven and in the earth. I heard many things in hell. How, then, am I mad? Hearken! and observe how healthily — how calmly I can tell you the whole story.
          It is impossible to say how first the idea entered my brain; but once conceived, it haunted me day and night. Object there was none. Passion there was none. I loved the old man. He had never wronged me. He had never given me insult. For his gold I had no desire. I think it was his eye! Yes, it was this! One of his eyes resembled that of a vulture — a pale blue eye, with a film over it. Whenever it fell upon me, my blood ran cold; and so by degrees — very gradually — I made up my mind to take the life of the old man, and thus rid myself of the eye for ever.
          Now this is the point. You fancy me mad. Madmen know nothing. But you should have seen me. You should have seen how wisely I proceeded — with what caution — with what foresight — with what dissimulation I went to

work! I was never kinder to the old man than during the whole week before I killed him. And every night, about midnight, I turned the latch of his door and opened it — oh, so gently! And then, when I had made an opening sufficient for my head, I put in a dark lantern, all closed, closed, so that no light shone out, and then I thrust in my head. Oh, you would have laughed to see how cunningly I thrust it in! I moved it slowly — very, very slowly, so that I might not disturb the old man's sleep. It took me an hour to place my whole head within the opening so far that I could see him as he lay upon his bed. Ha! — would a madman have been so wise as this? And then, when my head was well in the room, I undid the lantern cautiously — oh, so cautiously — cautiously (for the hinges creaked) — I undid it just so much that a single thin ray fell upon the vulture eye. And this I did for seven long nights — every night just at midnight — but I found the eye always closed; and so it was impossible to do the work; for it was not the old man who vexed me, but his Evil Eye. And every morning, when the day broke, I went boldly into the chamber, and spoke courageously to him, calling him by name in a hearty tone, and inquiring how he had passed the night. So you see he would have been a very profound old man, indeed, to suspect that every night, just at twelve, I looked in upon him while he slept.

1. In relation to the passage as a whole, the first sentence acts as a

    (A) definition of the passage

    (B) contradiction to the passage

    (C) setter of the pace

    (D) establishment of the mood

    (E) foreshadowing of upcoming events

2. By "I heard all things in heaven and in the earth" the author literally means he was

    (A) listening well

    (B) going crazy

    (C) slowly dying

    (D) an animal

    (E) home sick

3. In the second paragraph the old man's eye is described with adjectives that seem to make it

    (A) have a heroic sense

    (B) sound scary and frightening

    (C) seem like the man

    (D) appear a little happy

    (E) appear a little sad

4. In context dissimulation is best understood to mean

    (A) craftiness

    (B) show

    (C) concealment

    (D) understand

    (E) hardiness

5. Which of the following quotes is most likely an exaggeration?

    (A) "The disease had sharpened my senses"

    (B) "I heard all things in the heaven and in the earth."

    (C) "Passion there was none"

    (D) "For his gold I had no desire"

    (E) "I had made an opening sufficient for my head"

6. In context "vexed" (line 25) is best understood to mean

    (A) mollify

    (B) rapture

    (C) placate

    (D) hated

    (E) aspirate

7. The passage describes the responses of a(n)

    (A) happy man

    (B) mad man

    (C) obsessive man

    (D) sad man

    (E) lucky man

8. The author's attitude toward the eye can be best described as

    (A) love

    (B) aversion

    (C) despise

    (D) affinity

    (E) predilection

9. In the sentence " would a madman have been so wise" the speaker says

        (A) he is a madman
        (B) the madmen are smart
        (C) madmen are not wise
        (D) madmen are often very crazy
        (E) madmen are fictional human beings

10. The passage characterizes the speaker as

        (A) happy
        (B) melancholy
        (C) calm
        (D) suicidal
        (E) crazy

11. In this passage one prominent characteristic of the speakers style is his predominant use of

        (A) detail
        (B) simile
        (C) analogy
        (E) metaphors

12. In the context of the passage, the author probably intends the reader to find the words "madman" and "vulture eye"

        (A) sobering
        (B) deceptive
        (C) horrifying
        (D) humorous
        (E) compassionate

13. The effect that Poe was trying to achieve can best be described as all of the following EXCEPT

        (A) apprehension
        (B) repulsion
        (C) horror
        (D) revulsion
        (E) compassion

<u>Questions 14-26.</u> Read the following excerpt from Animal Farm by George Orwell carefully before you choose your answers.

Old Major cleared his throat and began to sing. As he had said, his voice was hoarse, but he sang well enough, and it was a stirring tune, something between Clementine and La Cucaracha. The words ran:

> Beasts of England, beasts of Ireland,
> Beasts of every land and clime,
> Hearken to my joyful tidings
> Of the golden future time.

5
> Soon or late the day is coming,
> Tyrant Man shall be o'erthrown,
> And the fruitful fields of England
> Shall be trod by beasts alone.

> Rings shall vanish from our noses,
10
> And the harness from our back,

> Bit and spur shall rust forever,
> Cruel whips no more shall crack.

> Riches more than mind can picture,
> Wheat and barley, oats and hay,
15
> Clover, beans, and mangel-wurzels
> Shall be ours upon that day.

> Bright will shine the fields of England,
> Purer shall its waters be,
> Sweeter yet shall blow its breezes
20
> On the day that sets us free.

> For that day we all must labour,
> Though we die before it break;
> Cows and horses, geese and turkeys,
> All must toil for freedom's sake.

25
> Beasts of England, beasts of Ireland,
> Beasts of every land and clime,
> Hearken well and spread my tidings
> Of the golden future time.

14. In the first stanza of the poem, the speaker's attitude toward the material in that of a person who is
      (A) relaxed
      (B) angered
      (C) controlled
      (D) determined
      (E) loved

15. In the first stanza, what does the poet mean by "Beasts"?
      (A) hogs
      (B) people
      (C) animals
      (D) pigs
      (E) cows

16. The first stanza and the last stanza repeats mainly to
      (A) convey an important meaning
      (B) bore readers to their graves
      (C) end the passage with a question
      (D) make up people's minds
      (E) create a strong sense of hostility

17. The "golden future time" (lines 4 and 28) refers to when
      (A) they overthrow man
      (B) they will climb
      (C) they get money
      (D) tomorrow will come
      (E) evil will reign

18. Which of the following is the grammatical antecedent of "our" (lines 9 and 10)?
      (A) men
      (B) fields
      (C) beasts
      (D) rings
      (E) harnesses

19. By "Cruel whips no more shall crack" (line 12) what was the main idea being stressed by the author by saying this?
      (A) We will not be whipped any more.
      (B) We will not be controlled anymore.
      (C) We will not have slavery anymore.
      (D) We will not lash out any more.
      (E) We will not be bad any more.

20. The principle function of the sentence "Riches more than the mind can picture" (line 13) is to represent
    (A) opportunity
    (B) wisdom
    (C) hatred
    (D) disturbance
    (E) structure

21. In context "Toil" (line 24) is best understood to mean
    (A) punishment
    (B) slavery
    (C) strain
    (D) ease
    (E) bondage

22. It can be inferred that "clime" (line 26) refers most specifically to
    (A) nature
    (B) culture
    (C) people
    (D) politics
    (E) mountains

23. The speaker's in this passage can be described as someone who is determined to
    (A) unite England and Ireland
    (B) conquer and overthrow man
    (C) live with all humans
    (D) have no luxuries
    (E) make good rulers of mankind

24. The speakers primary purpose in this passage is to
    (A) describe a series of unprecedented events
    (B) comment on a very popular assumption
    (C) characterize an idyllic era
    (D) give them united purpose for ambition
    (E) make people think they are bad

25. In this passage, one prominent characteristic of the poet's style is use of
    (A) logos
    (B) pathos
    (C) metaphors
    (D) oxymorons
    (E) allusions

26. The speaker's attitude toward man can best be described
as   (A) admiring
        (B) hating
        (C) discouraging
        (D) loving
        (E) caring

Questions 27-38. Read the following excerpt from "A Letter
from Captain Gulliver to his Cousin" by Jonathan Swift carefully before you choose your answers.

     I hope you will be ready to own publicly, when-
ever you shall be called to it, that by your great and frequent
urgency, you prevailed on me to publish a very loose and incorrect account of my travels; with direction to hire some
young gentleman of either university to put them in order, and
correct the style, as my Cousin Dampler did by my advice, in
his book called *A Voyage Around the World.* But, I do not remember, I gave you power to consent, that anything should
be omitted, and much less that anything should be inserted:
Therefore, as to the latter, I do here renounce everything of
that kind; particularly a paragraph about her majesty, the late
Queen Anne, of most pious and glorious memory; although I
did reverence and esteem her more than any of human spe-
cies. But you, or your interpolator, ought to have considered,
that as it was not my inclination, so was it not decent to praise
any animal of our composition before my master Hoyhnhnm:
and besides, the fact was altogether false, for, to my knowledge, being in England during some part of her majesty's reign,
she did govern by a chief minister; nay, even by two succes-
sively; the first whereof was the Lord of Godolphin, and the
second the Lord of Oxford; so that you have made me say the
thing which was not. Likewise, in the account of the Academy
of Projectors, and several passages of my discourse to my master Hoyhnhnm, you have either omitted some material circumstances, or minced or changed them in such a manner, that I
do hardly know mine own work. When I formally hinted to
you something of this in a letter, you were pleased to answer,
that you were afraid of giving offense; that people in power
were very watchful over the press; and apt not only to interpret, but to punish everything which looked like an innuendo
(as I think you called it). But pray, how could that which I

spoke so many years ago, and at above five thousand leagues distance, in another reign, be applied to any of the Yahoos, who are said to now govern the herd; especially at a time when I little thought on, or feared the unhappiness of living under them? Have not I the most reason to complain, when I see these very Yahoos carried by Hoyhnhnms in a vehicle as if these were brutes, and those the rational creatures? And, indeed, to avoid so monstrous and detestable a sight, was on principal motive of my retirement hither.

Thus much I thought proper to tell you in relation to yourself, and to the trust I reposed in you.

27. "I hope you will be ready to own publicly" (line 1) means
      (A) I hope you will admit your mistake to everyone
      (B) I hope you will tell the public you were right
      (C) I hope you keep your mouth shut
      (D) I hope you tell me you were right
      (E) I hope you will go out into the public

28. "The function of the first sentence is to
      (A) state the problem with Sympson's Book
      (B) make people think till their head falls off
      (C) make Sympson want to go with him on a trip
      (D) make Sympson feel bad about his mistakes
      (E) tell Sympson of Dumpier's Book

29. Early in the passage, Swift is attempting to satirize
      (A)   pointless travel logs
      (B) bad writing
      (C) the late Queen Anne.
      (D) the Queen's ministers
      (E) his cousin Sympson

30. The word "innuendo" (line 18) means
      (A) obvious statement
      (B) dramatic change
      (C) outright lie
      (D) outright praise
      (E) veiled allusion

31. In line 22, the antecedent of "them" is
      (A) Hoyhnhnms
      (B) Sympson
      (C) Yahoos.
      (D) Herders
      (E) Parliament

32. The tone of this passage is best described as
    (A) maddening
    (B) threatening
    (C) joking
    (D) pleasing
    (E) frustrating

33. In the passage the Yahoos are employed as a metaphor for
    (A) mankind
    (B) carriage drivers
    (C) horses
    (D) herders
    (E) Parliament

34. In the passage, Swift uses which of the following devices most often?
    (A) overstatement
    (B) allusion
    (C) satire
    (D) sarcasm
    (E) irony

35. The author's attitude toward the Hoyhnhnm can best be described as one of
    (A) Anger
    (B) Dislike
    (C) Disgust
    (D) Boredom
    (E) Praise

36. Gulliver's attitude toward his cousin is
    (A) displeasure because of false statements
    (B) happy for the work he did
    (C) hatred because Sympson is stupid
    (D) sarcastic about Sympson's job
    (E) disgusted about Sympson's character

37. Capt. Gulliver's point of view in his letter is
    (A) distant from his argument
    (B) displeasure at his cousin's writing
    (C) anger involved in the writing
    (D) disgust at the Late Queen's actions
    (E) passive viewing of the argument

Question 38 - 43. Read the following poem *On First Looking into Chapman's Homer* by John Keats carefully before choosing your answers.

On First Looking into Chapman's Homer

Much have I traveled in the realms of gold,
And many goodly states and kingdoms seen;
Round many western islands have I been
Which bards in fealty to Apollo hold.
(5) Oft of one wide expanse had I been told
That deep-browed Homer ruled as his demesne,
Yet did I never breathe its pure serene
Till I heard Chapman speak out loud and bold:
Then felt I like some watcher of the skies
(10) When a new planet swims into his ken;
Or like stout Cortez when with eagles eyes
He stared at the Pacific — and all his men
Looked at each other with a wild surmise —
Silent, upon a peak in Darien.

Line 4 - **Apollo** - Greek god of poetry . . . Line 6 - **demesne** - estate . . . Line 7 - **serene** - atmosphere . . . Line 10 - **ken** - range of sight . . . Line 11- **Cortez** - Vasco Nunez de Balboa, not Hernando Cortez, was the first European to sight the Pacific from Darien, a peak in Panama.

38. This poem is concerned with all of the following EXCEPT:
    (A) reading as a method of imaginative discovery
    (B) personal experience as a symbol for any discovery
    (C) Keats's personal discovery of Chapman's Homer
    (D) Cortez's discovery of the Pacific Ocean
    (E) the importance of imaginative discovery through
        reading
39. The controlling metaphor for discovery in the poem is built around a comparison of reading with
    (A) writing
    (B) traveling
    (C) science
    (D) physics
    (E) medicine

40. Written as a Italian sonnet, John Keats had to follow the formal organization established by all of the following rules for a sonnet EXCEPT:

    (A) The ideas in the poem must be expressed in 14 lines, no more or no less.

    (B) Each line has to consist of 10 syllables.

    (C) The meter has to be iambic pentameter.

    (D) The verse has to be unrhymed.

    (E) The sonnet has to be organized into two unequal parts, an octave and a sestet.

41. In an Italian sonnet the reader has certain expectations for how meaning will be formed. Which of the following possibilities have been chosen by John Keats?

    (A) The octave presents a problem, the sestet a solution.

    (B) The octave and the sestet present the same problem from two different views.

    (C) The problem of the octave is intensified in the sestet, and no solution is given.

    (D) The octave presents a situation and a sestet describes a change in the situation.

    (E) The octave and the sestet presents different types of changes.

42. In the octave, the speaker writes that he has " traveled in the realms of gold," and seen "many goodly states and kingdoms." Given the context of the rest of the poem, we know that the speaker is referring to his

    (A) wide reading in the literature of Western civilization

    (B) many travels to the western islands

    (C) vast study of our planet system

    (D) intense concern for the Preservation of eagles

    (E) accurate research on explorers

43. Examples of formal and dignified diction, used by John Keats to represent his respectful but dispassionate reading before discovering Chapman's Homer, include all BUT which of the following?

    (A) "goodly states"

    (B) "bards of fealty"

    (C) "had I been told"

    (D) "demesne"

    (E) "serene"

44. A "turn" occurs between the octave and the sestet when the speaker describes the impact that reading Chapman's Homer has had on him. Images of exploration give way to
    (A) more intensified images of exploration
    (B) images of discovery
    (C) questions about the necessity of exploration
    (D) answers to the questions about exploration previously made
    (E) excitement and awe at the wonders discovered through reading

45. The tone also changes from the octave's respectful but dispassionate assessment of reading to the sestet's
    (A) adulation and reverence for God's many wonders
    (B) smugness and self-satisfaction with human accomplishments
    (C) repugnance and disgust with the evil mortals enjoy
    (D) arrogance and contempt for Cortez's lack of accomplishments
    (E) excitement and awe at the wonders discovered through reading

46. The following similes are used in the concluding sestet to convey the speaker's changed attitude:
    I. He compares his enthusiasm to that of someone who has perhaps seen a new planet through a telescope.
    II. He compares his elation to that of an explorer who has seen an eagle in its wild habitat.
    III. He compares his astonishment to that of Cortez's

47. A calm and measured movement can be seen in the octave, but the sestet's movement conveys the speaker's heightened emotions. Keats reinforces this flurry of feelings by manipulating the syntax so that the predominant iambic pentameter is accompanied with
    (A) dashes and run-on lines
    (B) balanced sentences
    (C) periodic thoughts
    (D) compound-complex sentence structure
    (E) loose sentence construction

48. When the speaker refers to Hernando Cortez as a means of creating a visual representation of the emotional intensity experienced by the speaker, he is making use of which stylistic device?

    (A) personification

    (B) metonymy

    (C) oxymoron

    (D) allusion

    (E) metaphor

49. All BUT one of the following words are chosen by John Keats in the sestet to represent intensity:

    (A) "swims"

    (B) "eagle eyes"

    (C) "silent"

    (D) "wild surmise"

    (E) "deep-browed"

50. The sonnet ends leaving both the speaker and the explorer

    (A) stranded on a peak

    (B) lost in the Pacific Ocean

    (C) looking at each other

    (D) contemplating further discoveries

    (E) staring at the Pacific

A Closing Bonus:
Preparing for the
"Open Question"

Literature and Composition — AP

It is necessary to continue an extremely wide variety of reading in order to continue improving creative reading and successful writing skills. These skills will be tested in May in the form of a multiple choice test and two analysis questions, one on prose, and one on poetry. However, the Literature exam has an "open" question which requires a little bit different preparation — the close study of a longer work of fiction.

The Open question directs the writer to analyze the effectiveness of a specific element as seen in a work chosen by the student. To prepare for this, consider the literature you have already read, and fill in the criteria for those works on the following pages.

Title-Author of Novel Number One

Collect the type of specific data seen below for two twentieth century novels of literary merit that you were assigned as approved reading in your AP course:

Opening paragraphs: _____

_____

_____

_____

Teacher Check _____

Major Characters: _____

_____

_____

_____

Teacher Check _____

Inner or outer characters: _____

_____

_____

_____

Teacher Check _____

Thematic implications: _____

_____

_____

_____

Teacher Check _____

Prominent stylistic devices: _____

_____

_____

_____

Teacher Check _____

Notable Quotes_____

_____

_____

_____

Teacher Check _____

Title-Author of Novel Number Two

Collect the type of specific data seen below for two twentieth century novels of literary merit that you were assigned as approved reading in your AP course:

Opening paragraphs: _____

_____

_____

_____

Teacher Check _____

Major Characters: _____

_____

_____

_____

Teacher Check _____

Inner or outer characters: _____

_____

_____

_____

Teacher Check _____

Thematic implications: _____

_____

_____

_____

Teacher Check _____

Prominent stylistic devices: _____

_____

_____

_____

Teacher Check _____

Notable Quotes_____

_____

_____

_____

Teacher Check _____

Title-Author of Modern Play Number One

Collect the type of specific data seen below for two twentieth dramas of literary merit that you were assigned as approved reading in your AP course:

Opening and closing scenes: _____

_____
Teacher Check _____

Major actors and actresses: _____

_____
Teacher Check _____

Inner or outer characters: _____

_____
Teacher Check _____

Thematic implications: _____

_____
Teacher Check _____

Production devices: _____

_____
Teacher Check _____

Notable Quotes: _____

_____
Teacher Check _____

Title-Author of Modern Play Number Two

Collect the type of specific data seen below for two twentieth dramas of literary merit that you were assigned as approved reading in your AP course:

Opening and closing scenes: _____

_____
Teacher Check _____

Major actors and actresses: _____

_____
Teacher Check _____

Inner or outer characters: _____

_____
Teacher Check _____
Teacher Check _____

Modern Play Number Two (continued)

Thematic implications: _____

_____
                        Teacher Check _____
Production devices: _____

_____
                        Teacher Check _____
Notable Quotes: _____

_____
                        Teacher Check _____

_____

Title of Shakespeare Tragedy

Collect the type of specific data seen below for one Shakespearean tragedy that you were assigned as approved reading
in your AP course:

Notable Settings: _____

_____
                        Teacher Check _____
Major characters: _____

_____
                        Teacher Check _____
Rising and Falling Action: _____

_____
                        Teacher Check _____
Thematic implications: _____

_____
                        Teacher Check _____
Opening and Concluding Scenes: _____

_____
                        Teacher Check _____
Notable Quotes: _____

_____
                        Teacher Check _____

_____

Title of Shakespeare Comedy

Collect the type of specific data seen below for one Shakespeare comedy that you were assigned as approved reading in your AP course:

Notable Settings: _____

_____

Teacher Check _____

Major characters: _____

_____

Teacher Check _____

Rising and Falling Action: _____

_____

Teacher Check _____

Thematic implications: _____

_____

Teacher Check _____

Opening and Concluding Scenes: _____

_____

Teacher Check _____

Notable Quotes: _____

_____

Teacher Check _____

_____

Practice Test 3:
"Use A PEN"

ENGLISH
LITERATURE AND COMPOSITION
SECTION II
Time — 2 hours
Number of questions — 3
Percent of total grade — 55

Each question counts as one-third of the total essay score.
Question 1 Essay — Suggested time. . . . . 40 minutes
Question 2 Essay — Suggested time. . . . . 40 minutes
Question 3 Essay — Suggested time. . . . . 40 minutes

Section II of this examination requires answers in essay form. To help you use your time well, the coordinator will announce the time at which each question should be completed. If you finished any question before the time is announced, you may go on to the following question. If you finish the examination in less than the time allotted, you may go back and work on any essay you want.

The quality of the composition will be considered in the scoring of all essay questions. Essays will be judged on their clarity and effectiveness in dealing with the topics. In response to Question 3, select only a work of literary merit that will be appropriate to the question. A general rule of thumb is to use works of the same quality as those you have been reading during your Advanced Placements year(s).

After completing each question, you should check your essay for accuracy, punctuation, spelling, and diction; you are advised, however, not to attempt many long corrections. Remember that quality is far more important than quantity.

You should write your essays with a pen, preferably in black or dark blue ink. If you must use a pencil, be sure it has a well-sharpened point. Be sure to write CLEARLY and LEGIBLY. Cross out any errors you make.

The questions for Section II are printed in the green insert. Use the green insert to organize your answers and for scratch work, but write your answers in the pink essay booklet. Answer questions in order and number each answer as the question is numbered in the examination. Do not skip lines. Begin each answer on a new page in the pink essay booklet.

Note: These directions are copied from the essay section of *The 1994 AP English Literature and Composition: Free-Response Scoring Guide with Multiple-Choice Section* © Copyright 1995 by College Entrance Examination Board and Educational Testing Service. All rights reserved.

ENGLISH LITERATURE AND COMPOSITION
SECTION II

Total Time — 2 hours

Question 1

(Suggested time — 40 minutes. This question
counts one-third of the total)

Read the following excerpt from *Narrative of the Life of Frederick Douglass, An American Slave.* Then write a careful analysis of how the narrator reveals the character of Mr. Austin Gore. You may emphasize whichever literary techniques (e. g. tone, selection of detail, syntax - such as parallelism or balanced sentence structure - point of view, irony, imagery, diction, anecdote, choice of tense, and so forth) you find most significant.

Mr. Hopkins remained but a short time in the office of overseer. Why his career was so short, I do not know, but suppose he lacked the necessary severity to suit Colonel Lloyd. Mr. Hopkins was succeeded by Mr. Austin Gore, a man possessing, in an eminent degree, all those traits of character indispensable to what is called a first-rate overseer. Mr. Gore had served Colonel Lloyd, in the capacity of overseer, upon one of the out-farms, and had shown himself worthy of the high station of overseer upon the home or Great House Farm.

Mr. Gore was proud, ambitious, and persevering. He was artful, cruel, and obdurate. He was just the man for such a place, and it was just the place for such a man. It afforded scope for the full exercise of all his powers, and he seemed to be perfectly at home in it. He was one of those who could torture the slightest look, word, or gesture, on the part of the slave, into impudence, and would treat it accordingly. There must be no answering back to him; no explanation was allowed a slave, showing himself to have been wrongfully accused. Mr. Gore acted fully up to the maximum laid down by slaveholders — "It is better that a dozen slaves suffer under the lash, than that the overseer should be convicted, in the presence of the slaves, of having been at fault." No matter how innocent a slave might be — it availed him nothing, when accused by Mr. Gore of any misdemeanor. To be accused was to be convicted, and to be convicted was to be punished; the one always followed the other with immutable certainty. To escape punishment was to escape accusation; and few slaves had the fortune to do either, under the overseership of Mr. Gore. He was just proud enough to demand the most debasing homage of the slave, and quite servile enough to crouch, himself, at the feet of the master. He was ambitious enough to be contented with nothing short of the highest rank of overseers, and persevering enough to reach the height of his ambition. He was cruel enough to inflict the severest punishment, artful enough to descend to the lowest trickery, and obdurate enough to be insensible to the voice of a reproving conscience. He was, of all the overseers, the most dreaded by the slaves. His presence was painful; his eye flashed confusion; and seldom was his sharp, shrill voice heard, without producing horror and trembling in their ranks.

Mr. Gore was a grave man, and, though a young man, he indulged in no jokes, said no funny words, seldom smiled. His words were in perfect keeping with his looks, and his looks were in perfect keeping with his words. Overseer will sometimes indulge in a witty word, even with the slaves; not so with Mr. Gore. He spoke but to command, and commanded but to be obeyed; he dealt sparingly with his words, and bountifully with his whip, never using the former where the latter would answer as well. When he whipped, he seemed to do so from a sense of duty, and feared no consequences. He did nothing reluctantly, no matter how disagreeable; always at his post, never inconsistent. He never promised but to fulfill. He was, in a word, a man of the most inflexible firmness and stone-like coolness.

His savage barbarity was equalled only by the consummate coolness with which he committed the grossest and most savage deeds upon the slaves under his charge. Mr. Gore once undertook to whip one of Colonel Lloyd's slaves, by the name of Demby. He had given Demby but few stripes, when, to get rid of the scourging, he ran and plunged himself into the creek, and stood there at the depth of his shoulders, refusing to come out. Mr. Gore told him that he would give him three calls, and that, if he did not come out after the third call, he would shoot him. The first call was given. Demby made no response, but stood his ground. The second and third calls were given with the same result. Mr. Gore, then, without consultation or deliberation with anyone, not even giving Demby an additional call, raised his musket to his face, taking deadly aim at his standing victim, and in an instant poor Demby was no more. His mangled body sank out of sight, and blood and brains marked the spot where he had stood.

A thrill of horror flashed through every soul upon the plantation, excepting Mr. Gore. He alone seemed cool and collected. He was asked by Colonel Lloyd and my old master, why he resorted to this extraordinary expedient. His reply was (as well as I could remember), that Demby had become unmanageable. He was setting a dangerous example to the other slaves, — one which, if suffered to pass without some such demonstration on his part, would finally lead to the total subversion of all law and order on the plantation. He argued that if one slave refused to be corrected, and escaped with his life, the other slaves would soon copy his example; the result of which would be, the freedom of the slaves, and the enslavement of the whites. Mr. Gore's defence was satisfactory. He was continued in his station as overseer upon the home plantation. His fame as an overseer went abroad. His horrid crime was not even submitted to judicial investigation. It was committed in the presence of slaves, and they of course could neither institute a suit, nor testify against him; and thus the guilty perpetrator of one of the bloodiest and most foul murders goes unwhipped of justice, and uncensured by the community in which he lives. Mr. Gore lived in St. Michael's, Talbot county, Maryland, when I left there; and if he is still alive, he very probably lives there now; and if so, he is now, as he was then, as highly esteemed and as much respected as though his guilty soul had not been stained with his brother's blood.

Question 2
(Suggested time — 40 minutes. This question counts one-third of the total)

The following two poems are written about death and pride. Read the poems carefully. Then write a carefully reasoned essay in which you analyze how each poet manipulates the language to convey a somewhat similar view.

Death Be Not Proud

> Death be not proud, though some have called thee
> Mighty and dreadful, for thou art not so,
> For those whom thou think'st thou dost overthrow
> Die not, poor death, nor yet canst thou kill me;
> From rest and sleep, which but thy pictures be,
> Much pleasure, then from thee, much more must flow,
> And soonest our best men with thee do go,
> Rest of their bones, and soul's delivery.
> Thou art slave to fate, chance, kings, and desperate
>   men,
> And dost with poison, war, and sickness dwell,
> And poppy, or charms, can make us sleep as well,
> And better than thy stroke; why swellest thou then?
> One short sleep past, we wake eternally,
> And death shall be no more, Death thou shalt die.
>   John Donne
>   (1572-1631)

Ozymandias

I met a traveler from an antique land,
Who said — "Two vast and trunkless legs of stone
Stand in the desert . . . . Near them, on the sand,
Half sunk a shattered visage lies, whose frown,
And wrinkled lip, and sneer of cold command,
Tell that its sculptor well those passions read
Which yet survive, stamped on these lifeless things,
The hand that mocked them, and the heart that fed;
And on the pedestal, these words appear:
My name is Ozymandias, King of Kings,
Look on my works, ye mighty, and despair!
Nothing beside remains. Round the decay
Of that colossal wreck, boundless and bare
The lone and level sands stretch far away.

Percy Bysshe Shelly
(1792-1822)

Question 3

(Suggested time — 40 minutes. This questions counts one-third of the total essay score.)

Anton Chekhov indicated in a letter to A. S. Souvorin, October 27, 1888, that a writer should never confuse "solving a problem" with "stating a problem. It is only the second that is obligatory for the artist." It is the artists' duty to present the right questions; the answers must be given by the reader in their own light.

In an essay, discuss the ending of a work of literary merit. With Chekhov's philosophy in mind, discuss how significant closure requires that the reader abide by or adjust to ambiguity or uncertainty. Explain how or why the ending appropriately <u>or</u> inappropriately concludes the work. Do not merely summarize the plot.

Choose a novel or play by one of the following authors or another author of comparable merit.

Jane Austen	Carson McCullers
Joseph Conrad	Arthur Miller
George Eliot	Herman Melville
Louise Erdich	Toni Morrison
William Faulkner	Vladimir Nabokov
Henry Fielding	Sean O'Casey
Lorraine Hansberry	Eugene O'Neill
Thomas Hardy	Cynthia Ozick
Lillian Hellman	Harold Pinter
Zora Neal Hurston	Jean Rhys
Henry James	William Shakespeare
James Joyce	George Bernard Shaw
D. H. Lawrence	Jonathan Swift
Katherine Mansfield	Alice Walker
Eudora Welty	Edith Wharton

PRACTICE TEST 3 SCORING

NOTE: See separate teacher's guide for answers and explanations for all multiple-choice tests in this book. Add the results of your scores below to determine your AP Grade:

Section I: Multiple-Choice (Total)

_____ - (.25 X _____) = _____ X 1.35 =_____

| Number Correct | Number Wrong | Multiple-Choice Score | Weighted Score Section I |

Section II: Free-Response

Writing: Essay 1: _____ X 3.0556 = _____
Do not round

Writing: Essay 2: _____ X 3.0556 = _____
Do not round

Writing: Essay 3: _____ X 3.0556 = _____
Do not round

Use CHECKLISTS or RUBRICS on the preceding pages to grade your essays.

Weighted Section II Score

Do not round

Composite Score:

_____ + _____ = _____

| Weighted Multiple-Choice Score | Weighted Free-Response Score | **Composite** |

Composite Score	AP Grade
150 - 107 (71%)	5
106 - 93 (62%)	4
92 - 74 (49%)	3
73 - 44 (29%)	2
43 - 0	1

Answers and Explanations

To Practice Test 3: Section II: Essay

Checklist for
Question 1

from *Narrative of the Life of Frederick Douglass, An American Slave*
by Frederick Douglass

STEP 1:   Check each item listed below which accurately describes the positive aspects of the essay being graded. Add one point for each item checked from the list. This side describes the basic requirements for a well-written essay. (Grader one should check column one. Grader two should check column two):

___-___1. The writer demonstrates a perceptive understanding of Mr. Austin Gore's character.

___-___2. The writer analyzes how the author uses literary techniques (e. g. tone, selection of detail, syntax - such as parallelism or balanced sentence structure - point of view, irony, imagery, diction, anecdote, choice of tense, and so forth) to characterize Mr. Gore.

___-___3. The writer demonstrates a perceptive understanding of how the language is manipulated by Frederick Douglass to reveal Mr. Gore's character.

___-___4. The writer makes apt (a minimum of three embedded bits of quotes per paragraph) and specific (detailed and appropriate) reference to the texts.

___-___5. The writer offers a convincing interpretation of the power of the character sketch.

___-___6. The writer demonstrates an ability to read perceptively by saying something beyond the easy and obvious to grasp

___-___7. The writer demonstrates a control over the virtues of effective communication, including the language unique to literary criticism.

___-___8. The writer's organization is implicit and original, yet communicates a clear message.

___-___9. The writer's diction, sentence structure, and grammar aid in communicating a clear message.

MAXIMUM SCORE RESULTS: Grader 1 _____
MAXIMUM SCORE RESULTS: Grader 2 _____

STEP 2: Check each item below which accurately describes the negative aspects of the essay being graded. This side describes how the essay may not be as good as the higher-scoring essays. (Grader one should check column one. Grader two should check column two):

___-___1. The writer's definition of Mr. Gore's personality is oversimplified or vague.

___-___2. The writer discusses the use of tone, selection of detail, syntax - such as parallelism or balanced sentence structure - point of view, irony, imagery, diction, anecdote, choice of tense, and so forth with limited purpose or with inappropriate examples.

___-___3. The connection between language and characterization is less clear than those of the top-scoring essays.

___-___4. The writer's use of quotes is awkward, inappropriate, or uninteresting.

___-___5. The writer's interpretation does not address the powerful effect of Mr. Gore's character .

___-___6. The writer displays simplistic thinking.

___-___7. The writer misuses the literary term(s) addressed in the question or omits them partially or entirely.

___-___8. The organization of this essay is less original or implicit than those of the top-scoring essays.

___-___9. The essay reveals consistent weakness in grammar and/or other basic elements of composition.

RESULTS:

Grader 1: _____ - _____ = _____
                  Step 1 Score   Step 2 Score

Grader 2: _____ - _____ = _____
                  Step 1 Score   Step 2 Score

Grader 1 Score + Grader 2 Score = _____

Above sum /
divided by 2 =

Score for essay

Answers and Explanations

To Practice Test 3:
Section II: AP Rubrics

Rubrics for Question 1

from *Narrative of the Life of Frederick Douglass, An American Slave* by Frederick Douglass

8-9   With apt and specific references to the story, the students who wrote these well-organized and well-written essays clearly analyze how Frederick Douglass uses literary techniques (e. g. tone, selection of detail, syntax - such as parallelism or balanced sentence structure - point of view, irony, imagery, diction, anecdote, choice of tense, and so forth) to characterize Mr. Gore. The best of these essays will acknowledge and then address the complexity of the characterization. While not without flaws, these papers will demonstrate an understanding of the text as well as consistent control over the elements of effective composition. These writers read with perception and express their ideas with clarity and skill.

6-7   Students who wrote these papers also analyze how Frederick Douglass uses literary techniques to characterize Mr. Gore, but they are less incisive, developed, or aptly supported than those who wrote papers in the highest range. They deal accurately with technique as a means by which a writer brings a character to life, but they are less effective or less thorough in their analysis than are the essays that score an 8 or 9. These essays demonstrate the writer's ability to express ideas clearly, but they do so with less maturity and precision than the best papers.

5   Students who wrote these essays respond to the assignment without important errors in composition, but they miss the complexity of Douglass's use of literary techniques and offer a perfunctory analysis of how those techniques are used to characterize Mr. Gore. Often, the analysis is vague, mechanical, superficial or inadequately supported. While the writing is sufficient to convey the writer's thoughts, these essays are not as well-conceived, organized, or developed as the upper-half papers. Usually, they reveal simplistic thinking and/or immature writing.

3-4   Students who wrote these lower-half essays reflect an incomplete understanding of the story and fail to respond adequately to the question. The discussion of how Douglass uses literary techniques to characterize Mr. Gore may be inaccurate or unclear, misguided or underdeveloped; these papers may paraphrase rather than analyze. The analysis of technique will likely be meager and unconvincing. Generally, the writing demonstrates weak control of such elements as diction, organization, syntax, or grammar. These essays typically contain recurrent stylistic flaws and/or misreadings and lack persuasive evidence from the text.

1-2   Students who wrote these essays compound the weaknesses of the prose of essays scoring a 3 or 4. They seriously misunderstand the character or fail to respond to the question. Frequently, they are unacceptably brief. Often poorly written on several counts, they may contain many distracting errors in grammar and mechanics. Although some attempt may have been made to answer the question, the writer's views typically are presented with little clarity, organization, coherence, or supporting evidence. Essays that are especially inexact, vacuous, and/or mechanically unsound should be scored 1.

0   This is a response with no more than a reference to the task.

-    Indicates a blank response, or one that is completely off the topic.

Answers and Explanations

To Practice Test 3:
Section II: Results
of Essay 1

from *Narrative of the Life of Frederick Douglass, An American Slave*
by Frederick Douglass

Following are examples of how the writer could demonstrate
a perceptive understanding of Mr. Austin Gore's character, analyzing how the author uses literary techniques (e. g. tone, selection of detail, syntax - such as parallelism or balanced sentence structure - point of view, irony, imagery, diction, anecdote, choice of tense, and so forth) to characterize Mr. Gore.

> A. Douglass's initial choice of positive diction ironi-
> cally are used in a negative sense as the character
> sketch is developed.
> B. Douglas uses an ambiguous point-counter point
> organization showing how Mr. Gore is respectful and
> civil in his white world, yet harsh and cruel as an over-
> seer.
> C. The passage is littered with condemning anecdotes
> that contrast with the positive generalizations of Gore.
> D. Rearranging words and varying sentence struc-
> ture allows Mr. Douglass to draw readers in, letting
> them experience his drastically changing impressions
> of the overseer, Mr. Austin Gore.

Following are examples of how the writer could make apt (a
minimum of three embedded bits of quotes per paragraph)
and specific (detailed and appropriate) reference to the text,
offering a convincing interpretation of Douglass's sketch.

> A. Gore held the ambition to become the best over-
> seer -- "persevering" to "reach the height of his ambi-
> tion."
> B. Mr. Gore's voice was seldom heard "without pro-
> ducing horror and trembling in their ranks."
> C. Ironically, Mr. Gore remained highly esteemed, as
> if "his guilty soul had not been stained with his
> brother's blood."

Following are example of how the writer could demonstrate an ability to read perceptively by saying something beyond the easy and obvious to grasp.

> A. Douglass paints an initially objective picture of Mr. Gore as a character striving for achievement in a harsh and cruel environment.
>
> B. In essence, Douglass's portrait of Mr. Gore is a 3D picture, respecting him for his "sense of duty," pitying him for his "inflexible firmness," and hating him for his "savage barbarity."

Do not force the same organization into every essay. Avoid topic sentences that name the device and make a connection to the view, yet say nothing specific or misread Douglass's revelation of Gore's character..

> A. Douglass's use of positive words conveyed that he thought highly of Mr. Gore. (This misreads Douglass's view.)
>
> B. Douglass uses syntax to reveal Mr. Gore's character. (B and C say nothing specific or meaningful.)
>
> C. Douglass uses parallelism and balanced sentence structure to reveal Mr. Gore's demeanor.

Rather, the writer's organization should be implicit and original, yet communicating a clear message. The highest scores will discuss the language of the passage in a natural way, attaching an individual interpretation to the writing .

> A. Although Douglass appears to respect Gore at first, it becomes increasingly clear that his attitude is quite the opposite.
>
> B. Mr. Austin Gore, a first-rate overseer, worthy of a high station like that of the overseer of the Great House Farm, lacked a guiltless soul.

Correct the following typical misuse of diction, sentence structure, and grammar:

> A. There are many descriptive adjectives of Gore's personality both with positive and negative connotations.
>
> B. Depending upon many different factors, such as race, religion and background experience, everyone has unique perceptions of someone's personality.
>
> C. In Douglass's excerpt, an American slave, Douglass's life story is relayed, where he lived, and the place he encountered.

Answers and Explanations

To Practice Test 3:
Section II: Essay

Checklist for Question 2
from John Donne's "Death Be Not Proud" and
Percy Bysshe Shelly's "Ozmandias"

STEP 1:   Check each item listed below which accurately describes the positive aspects of the essay being graded. Add one point for each item checked from the list. This side describes the basic requirements for a well-written essay. (Grader one should check column one. Grader two should check column two):

___-___1. The definition of the speakers' views of pride and death demonstrate a perceptive understanding of each of the works.

___-___2. The essay analyzes how such rhetorical or stylistic devices as figurative language, imagery, and irony are used differently by each author to convey a somewhat similar view.

___-___3. The essay continually shows the connection between the speakers' attitudes and the language devices used to convey that attitude.

___-___4. The essay supports the discussion of each language device with apt (a minimum of three embedded bits of quotes per paragraph) and specific (detailed and appropriate) reference to the both poems.

___-___5. Though not without flaws, these papers offer a convincing interpretation of both poems.

___-___6. The essay demonstrates the writer's ability to read perceptively .

___-___7. The writer demonstrates a control over the virtues of effective communication, including the language unique to literary criticism.

___-___8. The writer's organization is implicit and original, yet communicates a clear message.

___-___9. The writer's diction, sentence structure, and grammar aid in communicating a clear message.

MAXIMUM SCORE RESULTS: Grader 1 _____
MAXIMUM SCORE RESULTS: Grader 2 _____

STEP 2: Check each item below which accurately describes the negative aspects of the essay being graded. This side describes how the essay may not be as good as the higher-scoring essays. (Grader one should check column one. Grader two should check column two):

___-___1. The writer fails to respond adequately to part(s) of the question by simply defining the attitude, or simply naming the language devices used, or both.

___-___2. The writer's discussion of how such devices as figurative language, imagery, and irony are used differently by each author to convey a somewhat similar view may be vague, mechanical, or inadequately supported.

___-___3. The connection between the evidence and the authors' probable or intended attitudes becomes lost.

___-___4. Although adequate in number, the evidence in this essay is not as convincing as that of the top scoring essays. In addition, their analysis is likely to be less persuasive.

___-___5. The writer simply paraphrases each poem or has minor flaws in interpretation.

___-___6. The writer deals with the assigned task without major flaws, but has little to say beyond what is easy and obvious to grasp.

___-___7. The writer demonstrates uncertain control over the qualities of college-level composition.

___-___8. While the writing is sufficient to convey the writer's thoughts, these essays are not as well-conceived, organized, or developed as the upper half papers.

___-___9. The essay reveals consistent weakness in grammar and/or other basic elements of composition. Often they reveal simplistic thinking and/or immature writing.

RESULTS:

Grader 1: _____ - _____ = _____
           Step 1 Score   Step 2 Score

Grader 2: _____ - _____ = _____
           Step 1 Score   Step 2 Score

Grader 1 Score + Grader 2 Score = _____

Above sum /
divided by 2 =

Score for essay

Answers and Explanations

To Practice Test 3:
Section II: AP Rubrics

Rubrics for Question 2

from John Donne's "Death Be Not Proud" and
Percy Bysshe Shelly's "Ozymandias"

8-9   The students who wrote these well-written essays clearly demonstrate an understanding of how each author manipulates the language to convey a somewhat similar
view of pride and death. With apt and specific reference, they
analyze how such elements as figurative language, imagery,
and irony are used differently by each poet to convey a somewhat similar view. Though not without flaws, these papers
offer convincing interpretations of both poems; they demonstrate the writer's ability to read perceptively and write with
clarity and skill.

6-7   These essays also demonstrate an understanding of the somewhat similar view of pride and death, but compared to the best essays, they are less thorough or less precise
in analyzing the differences between the use of such devices
as figurative language, imagery, and irony. In addition to minor flaws in interpretation, their analysis is likely to be briefer,
less well-supported, and less incisive. These essays demonstrate the writer's ability to express ideas clearly, but with less
mastery and control than do papers scoring an 8 or 9.

5   The students who wrote these essays deal
with the assigned task without major errors, but have little to
say beyond what is easy and obvious to grasp. Their understanding of how such devices as figurative language, imagery,
and irony contribute to the views may be vague, mechanical,
superficial, or inadequately supported. While the writing is
sufficient to convey the writer's thoughts, these essays are not
as well conceived, organized or developed as the upper-half
papers. Often they reveal simplistic thinking and/or immature writing.

3-4   The students who wrote these lower-half essays fail to respond adequately to part(s) of the question. They reflect an incomplete understanding of the somewhat similar view of pride and death seen in each poem, and/or their treatment of such language devices such as figurative language, imagery, and irony may be meager or unclear, inaccurate or irrelevant. The writing usually demonstrates uncertain control over the qualities of college-level composition. They usually contain recurrent stylistic flaws and/or misreadings and lack persuasive evidence from the text. These essays may paraphrase rather than analyze. Essays scoring a 3 exhibit more than one of the problems explained above; they are marred by significant misinterpretations, insufficient development, or serious omissions.

1-2   The students who wrote these essays compound the weaknesses of the prose of essays scoring a 3 or 4. These writers seriously misread one or both of the poems. Frequently, they are unacceptably brief. Often poorly written on several counts, they may contain many distracting errors in grammar and mechanics. Although some attempt may have been made to answer the question, the writer's views typically are presented with little clarity, organization, coherence, or supporting evidence. Essays that are especially inexact, vacuous, and/or mechanically unsound should be scored 1.

0   This is a response with no more than a reference to the task.

-    Indicates a blank response, or one that is completely off the topic.

Answers and Explanations

To Practice Test 3:
Section II: Results
of Essay 2

from John Donne's "Death Be Not Proud" and
Percy Bysshe Shelly's "Ozymandias"

Following are examples of how the writer's definition of the
speakers' views of pride and death could demonstrate a perceptive understanding of each of the works, showing how such
rhetorical or stylistic devices as figurative language, imagery,
and irony are used differently by each author to convey a somewhat similar view.

> B. Although both poets view pride as a sinful trait,
> Donne addresses death directly, chastising it for hav-
> ing pride.
> A. Shelly, on the other hand, uses a story of the dead
> Pharaoh, Ozmandias, whose monuments of pride have
> been destroyed by the sands of time, to portray this
> more subtly.
> C. In both cases, death is viewed, respectively, as
> unimportant or as a means of showing unimportance.

Following are examples of how the writer could support the
discussion of each language device with apt (a minimum of
three embedded bits of quotes per paragraph) and specific (detailed and appropriate) reference to the both poems, offering a
convincing interpretation of both poems:

> A. Donne remarks that some have called death
> "mighty and dreadful," making people a "slave to fate."

> B. All that if left of Ozmandias's once great empire is
> "lone and level sand."

Do not force the same organization into every essay. Avoid topic sentences like those below that name the device and make a connection to the view, yet say nothing specific.

> A. Imagery is used to convey a similar view of death.
> B. Irony is used to covey a similar view of death.
> C. Figurative language is used to covey a similar view of death.
> D. Diction is an important element used by each poet to convey meaning.

Rather, the writer's organization should be implicit and original, yet communicating a clear message. The highest scores will discuss the language of the passage in a natural way, attaching an individual interpretation to the writing .

> A. Both poets indicate that death implies a certain loneliness for those whose pride is too excessive. (Note how this topic sentence addresses meaning. The rest of the paragraph would show how the poet manipulates the language to convey loneliness.)
> B. Both poets make ironic, almost satirical comments about death. (Note how this topic sentence addresses meaning. The rest of the paragraph would show how the poet manipulates the language to convey satire.)

Correct the following typical student mistakes involving misuse of diction, sentence structure, and grammar.

> A. There are millions of ways to express many types of feelings about death.
> B. In the poem by John Donne, he is expressing why death should not be proud.
> C. Death is looked upon in different ways by different people all around the world as a beginning of a new life or an ending to a perfect life.
> D. Both Donne and Shelly think that death is not a big deal like others make it out to be, only they use different techniques to express this thought.
> E. Both of the authors which wrote "Death Be Not Proud" and Ozmandias" view death a pride similarly.

Answers and Explanations

To Practice Test 3:
Section II: Essay

Checklist for Question 3

Open Question on AMBIGUITY OR UNCERTAINTY

STEP 1:   Check each item listed below which accurately describes the positive aspects of the essay being graded. Add one point for each item checked from the list. This side describes the basic requirements for a well-written essay. (Grader one should check column one. Grader two should check column two):

___-___1. The writer selects a suitable novel or play in which significant closure requires that the reader abide by or adjust to ambiguity or uncertainty.

___-___2. The writer presents a reasonable explanation of the meaning of the work.

___-___3. The writer effectively explains how or why the ending appropriately or inappropriately concludes the work.

___-___4. The writer convincingly explains the ending's significance to the work as a whole.

___-___5. The writer makes apt and specific reference to the text.

___-___6. The writer avoids plot summary not relevant to the explanation of the role that the ending plays in the evocation of multiple meanings in the work.

___-___7. The writer discusses the literary work with sophistication, insight, and understanding.

___-___8. The writer displays consistent control over the language unique to literary discussion.

___-___9. The writer's diction, sentence structure, organization, and grammar aid in communicating a clear message.

MAXIMUM SCORE RESULTS: Grader 1 _____
MAXIMUM SCORE RESULTS: Grader 2 _____

STEP 2: Check each item below which accurately describes the negative aspects of the essay being graded. This side describes how the essay may not be as good as the higher-scoring essays. (Grader one should check column one. Grader two should check column two):

___-___1. The writer's selection of a play or novel is not as appropriate as those of the higher-scoring essays.

___-___2. The writer's explanation of the meaning of the work is less thorough, less specific, or less perceptive than those of the higher-scoring essays.

___-___3. The writer's explanation of the appropriateness or inappropriateness of the selected work's ending may be vague, underdeveloped, or misguided.

___-___4. The writer's explanation of the ending's significance may be less convincing, mechanical, or inadequately related to the work as a whole.

___-___5. The writer's reference to the text lacks the specificity of the higher-scoring essays.

___-___6. The writer simply paraphrases the meaning of the work with little reference to how the ending's ambiguity or uncertainty elicits multiple meanings in the work.

___-___7. The writer says nothing beyond the easy and obvious to grasp.

___-___8. The writer misuses the literary term(s) necessary to literary discussion or omits them partially or entirely.

___-___9. The essay contains distracting errors in grammar and mechanics.

RESULTS:

Grader 1: _____ - _____ = _____
             Step 1 Score   Step 2 Score

Grader 2: _____ - _____ = _____
             Step 1 Score   Step 2 Score

Grader 1 Score + Grader 2 Score = _____

Above sum /
divided by 2 =

Score for essay

Answers and Explanations

To Practice Test 3:
Section II: AP Rubrics

Rubrics for Question 3

Open Question on AMBIGUITY OR UNCERTAINTY

8-9   The students who wrote these well-written essays identify the "ambiguity or uncertainty" evident in the ending of a novel or play of literary merit, and they explain convincingly its significance to the work as a whole. These essays will be specific in their references to the text, cogent in their explications, and free of plot summary not related to how significant closure requires that the reader abide by or adjust to ambiguity or uncertainty. These essays need not be without error, but they exhibit the writer's ability to discuss a literary work with insight and understanding, as well as the writer's ability to control an appropriate range of the elements of effective composition.

6-7   These essays also identify the "ambiguity or uncertainty" evident in the ending of a novel or play of literary merit. In addition, they explain the significance of that ending to the work as a whole. Their analysis, however, is less thorough, less perceptive, or less specific than the prose of essays scoring an 8 or 9. Though not as convincing in their discussion, these essays are generally well written. They demonstrate the writer's ability to explain how an ending of the kind Chekhov describes works relative to the novel or play as a whole, but they are less sophisticated in their analysis and less consistent in their command of the elements of effective college-level expository prose than are essays scoring an 8 or 9.

5   The students who wrote these essays may choose an appropriate ending, but their explanation of how significant closure requires that the reader abide by or adjust to ambiguity or uncertainty is vague, oversimplified, or superficial. Their discussion of meaning may also be pedestrian or mechanical. Typically, these essays reveal unsophisticated thinking and/or immature writing. They usually demonstrate inconsistent control over the elements of effective composition and are not as well conceived, organized, or developed as upper-half papers. The writing, however, is adequate to convey the writer's views.

3-4   The students who wrote these lower-half essays may not choose an ending that creates "ambiguity or uncertainty," or they may have failed to explain the significance of that ending to the work as a whole. Their analysis may be unpersuasive, perfunctory, underdeveloped, or misguided. Often, their discussion is inaccurate or not clearly related to the question. The writing may convey the writer's ideas, but it reveals weak control over such elements as the language unique to literary discussion, diction, organization, syntax, or grammar. These essays may contain important misinterpretations of the novel or play, inadequate supporting evidence, and/or use paraphrase and plot summary rather than analysis.

1-2   The student who wrote these essays compound the weaknesses of the papers scoring a 3 or 4. The writers seriously misread the play or novel, or seriously misinterpret the ending they have chosen. Frequently, they are unacceptably brief. Often poorly written on several counts, they may contain many distracting errors in grammar and mechanics. Although some attempt may have been made to answer the question, the writer's views typically are presented with little clarity, organization, coherence, or supporting evidence. Essays that are especially vacuous, ill-organized, illogically argued, and/or mechanically unsound should be scored 1.

0   This is a response with no more than a reference to the task.

-          Indicates a blank response, or one that is wholly unrelated to the assignment.

A Final Thought on the Power of Words
"PUNCH, BROTHERS, PUNCH" by Mark Twain

Will the reader please cast his eye over the following lines, and see if he can discover anything harmful in them?

> Conductor, when you receive a fare,
> Punch in the presence of the passenjare!
> A blue trip slip for an eight-cent fare,
> A buff trip slip for a six-cent fare,
> A pink trip slip for a three-cent fare,
> CHORUS
> Punch, brothers! punch with care!
> Punch in the presence of the passenjare!

I came across these jingling rhymes in the newspaper a little while ago and read them a couple of times. They took instant and entire possession of me. All through breakfast they went waltzing through my brain; and when, at last, I rolled up the napkin, I could not tell whether I had eaten anything or not. I had carefully laid out my day's work the day before — a thrilling tragedy in the novel which I am writing. I went to my den — my deed of blood. I took up my pen, but all I could get it to say was "Punch in the presence of the passenjare!" I fought hard for an hour but it was useless. My head kept humming, "A blue trip slip for an eight-cent fare, A buff trip slip for a six-cent fare," and so on and so on, without peace or respite. The day's work was ruined — I could see plainly enough. I gave up and drifted downtown, and presently discovered that my feet were keeping time to that relentless jingle. When I could stand it no longer, I altered my step. But it did no good; those rhymes accommodated themselves to the new step and went on harassing me just as before. I returned home and suffered all the afternoon; suffered all through an unconscious and unrefreshing dinner; suffered, and cried, and jingled all through the evening; went to bed and rolled, tossed, and jingled right along, the same as ever; got up at midnight frantic and tried to read; but there was nothing visible upon the whirling page except, "Punch! punch in the presence of the passenjare." By sunrise I was out of my mind, and everybody marveled and was distressed at the idiotic burden of my ravings — "Punch! oh, punch! punch in the presence of the passenjare!"

Two days later on a Saturday morning, I arose, a tottering wreck, and went forth to fulfill an engagement with a valued friend. . . . Mr. ___ talked, talked, talked — as is his wont. . . . At the end of a mile , Mr. ___ said:

"Mark, are you sick? I never in my life saw a man so haggard and worn, and absent-minded. Say something, do!"

. . . . I began at the beginning and repeated all the lines.

My friend's face lighted with interest. He said: "Why what a captivating jingle it is! It is almost music. It flows along so nicely. I have nearly caught the rhymes myself. Say them over just once more, and then I'll have them, sure."

I said them over. Then Mr. ___ said them. He made one little mistake, which I corrected. The next time and the next he got them right. Now a great burden seemed to tumble from my shoulders. That torturing jingle departed out of my brain, and a grateful sense of rest and peace descended upon me. I was light-hearted enough to sing; and I did sing for half an hour, straight along, as we went jogging homeward. Then my freed tongue found blessed speech again, and the pent talk of many a weary hour began to gush and flow. It flowed on and on, joyously, jubilantly, until the fountain was empty and dry. As I wrung my friend's hand at parting, I said: "Haven't we had a royal good time! But now I remember, you haven't said a word for two hours. Come, come, out with something."

The Rev. Mr. ___ turned a lackluster eye upon me, drew a deep sigh, and said, without animation, without apparent consciousness: "Punch, brothers, punch with care! Punch in the presence of the passenjare!"

A pang shot through me as I said to myself, "Poor fellow, poor fellow! *he* has got it, now."

I did not see Mr. ___ for two or three days after that. Then, on Tuesday evening, he staggered into my presence and sat dejectedly into a seat. He was pale, worn; he was a wreck.

. . . . How did I finally save him from an asylum? I took him to a neighboring university and made him discharge the burden of his persecuting rhymes into the eager ears of the poor, unthinking students. How is it with *them* now? The result is too sad to tell. Why did I write this article? It was for a worthy, even a noble purpose. It was to warn you, reader, if you should come across those merciless rhymes, to avoid them — avoid them as you would the pestilence!

SCHOOL HOUSE BOOKS

Date ____-____-____ Purchase Order Number _____

SHIP TO:

_____
Name of High School

_____
Contact Name

_____
Street Address / PO Box

_____
City, State Zip

BILL TO:

_____
Independent School District #

_____
Contact Name or Department

_____
Street Address / PO Box

_____
City, State Zip

**For Rush Orders Call 1•218•850•8981 or
Email at schoolhousebooks@lakesnet.net**

ITEM # PRODUCT	PRICE PER COPY	QUANTITY	TOTAL
4001 *A Practical AP Language Guide* (2nd ed.)	24.95	_____	_____
4002 AP LANGUAGE ANS/EXPLANATIONS	7.00	_____	_____
5001 *A Practical AP Literature Guide* (2nd ed.)	24.95	_____	_____
5002 AP LITERATURE ANS/EXPLANATIONS	7.00	_____	_____
6001 *School House Books WRITER* (1st ed.)	34.95	Available September 1999	
6002 *WRITER* ANS/EXPLANATIONS	7.00	Available September 1999	
7001 *School House Books READER* (2nd ed.)	44.95	Available September 1999	
7002 *READER* ANS/EXPLANATIONS	7.00	Available September 1999	

- -

SUBTOTAL _____

Subtract 10% (20% for 5 or more books)
                         Education Discount from Subtotal _____

Applicable Sales Tax _____

Shipping & Handling ($7.00 Minimum,
7-25 items = $1.00 per item, Larger Orders= Cost) _____

Please make check payable to:

**School House Books
921 Pembina Trail
Detroit Lakes, MN 56501**   **TOTAL** _____